WALKING THE
YORKSHIRE
COAST
• A COMPANION GUIDE •

Text and photographs by Chris Gee

PiXZ

First published in Great Britain in 2016

Text © 2016 Chris Gee

Every attempt has been made by the author and
publisher to secure the appropriate permissions
for materials reproduced in this book. If there
has been any oversight we will be happy to
rectify the situation in future editions, following a
written submission to the Publishers.

A CIP catalogue record for this book is available
from the British Library.

ISBN 978 0 85710 107 5

PiXZ Books
Halsgrove House, Ryelands Business Park,
Bagley Road, Wellington, Somerset TA21 9PZ
Tel: 01823 653777
Fax: 01823 216796
email: sales@halsgrove.com

An imprint of Halstar Ltd, part of the
Halsgrove group of companies
Information on all Halsgrove titles is
available at: www.halsgrove.com

Printed in China by
Everbest Printing Investment Ltd

*With thanks to my dad Tom
who instilled in me a love of travel
and adventure and with whom I
have walked much of this coast.
Thanks also to my wife Jo for
accompanying me on day trips
to the coast, for her patience
when waiting for the sun to come
back out again and for her
proofreading of the text.*

Front cover: *North Landing, Flamborough Head.*

CONTENTS

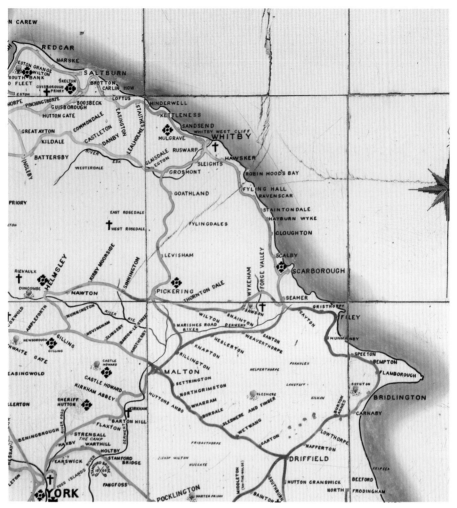

North Eastern Railway tile map, Filey railway station.

INTRODUCTION

One thing I like about Yorkshire is its variety. It's a huge county and in many ways, Yorkshire is a microcosm of England: high peaks; rolling countryside; chocolate box villages; pretty market towns; heather moorland and tumbling rivers. There are some that say that if you live in Yorkshire, you've no need to go on holiday to the rest of the British Isles, it can all be found here in England's largest county.

The thing I like most about Yorkshire though is the coast and for much the same reason: it offers real variety. There are Victorian seaside towns like Filey, Scarborough and Saltburn, the very epitome of the classic English seaside resort. There are quaint fishing harbours like Staithes, Runswick Bay and Robin Hood's Bay, as attractive and engaging as anything you'd find in Devon and Cornwall. There are high chalk cliffs, just like you find in Kent, Sussex and Dorset and so highly symbolic of the English coast. There are fine seabird colonies where you can find gannets, puffins, razorbills, guillemots and kittiwakes. Here, the smell and the sound, as well as the sight, is overwhelming, as good a wildlife spectacle as you might find on Bass Rock, Skomer Island or the Inner Hebrides. Grey seals haul out on rocks and from Whitby you can go whale watching in late summer in search of minke whales, harbour porpoise and bottlenose dolphins.

Then there is the heather moorland, a blaze of purple in late summer, which rolls down to almost touch the coast on the edge of the North York Moors, where adders and slow worms can be found basking on a summer's day.

There is evidence of industry too, past and present, the steel industry, mining, quarrying, fishing and railways.

East Scar and distant Bempton Cliffs from Flamborough Cliffs Nature Reserve.

Sunrise over Flamborough Head from Coble Landing, Filey.

There is constant change. Coastal erosion on parts of the Yorkshire coast happens at the fastest rate in Europe.

And then there is Whitby, a place of legend, atmosphere and history too, from where Captain Cook went on to explore the wider world and where Bram Stoker was inspired to write his classic Gothic novel, *Dracula*.

Almost the entire coastline is accessible, with long distance coastal paths that follow the very edge of Yorkshire. Those accessible sections are certainly the most appealing stretches of this spectacular coast. Some of these paths are National Trails like The Cleveland Way or other more recent long distance paths like The Headland Way. Others are ordinary, everyday footpaths which give access to some stunning, secret places. In spring and summer the coastal footpaths are a riot of colour, the pink of thrift and red campion, dazzling white ox eye daisies and cow parsley, bright yellow bird's foot trefoil and kidney vetch.

Our journey will take us south to north. I thought long and hard about whether to arrange the book as north to south or south to north. Initially north to south seemed logical, as one might read down a page and in most cases, the prevailing downhill gradient is north to south, but then I realised that the most impressive views are seen looking north, with the sun behind you, lighting up the view and the route ahead. That means that the journey described is therefore generally uphill – but surely that is one of the pleasures of walking, to spend the day climbing to higher ground to be rewarded with a stunning view that repays all that effort!

It matters not which way you tackle the Yorkshire coastal route, the public transport options are equally good in either direction and the footpaths and bridleways generally well signposted. The route described is a continuous 70 miles from Barmston to Saltburn.

Our journey starts in Barmston, just south of Bridlington and finishes in Saltburn at the end of the pier. I've walked it all, sometimes alone, mostly with my dog, my wife, my dad and my cousin and I never tire of it. I love to return in the various seasons, in spring and summer when the flowers are in bloom and the birds are busy, and in autumn and winter when most of the crowds have gone and the wild weather can bring high drama to the rolling sea.

I've omitted the section between Barmston and Spurn Point. I've walked some of this section too, but access isn't as easy, it is largely devoid of rights of way, requires long sections of road or beach walking and the scenery is less inspiring. The coast in this section is ever changing, ever eroding, as each storm bites huge chunks of boulder clay out of the East Riding coast. I guess this section is for obsessive completists only, who are happy to plan their walk around the tides. Spurn Point is well worth a visit in its own right and it is possible to walk the length of the point, but between Barmston and Spurn, perhaps the only highlights are Hornsea and Withernsea and the area around Skipsea.

For similar reasons I've left out the section from Saltburn Pier to Gare Point and the mouth of the River Tees. Again there are few rights of way and the route mostly involves walking along the beach or promenade through Redcar and Marske against a backdrop of the steelworks, blast furnaces and coking plants of industrial Teesside. Marske is worth a visit and it's an easy walk from Saltburn along the sands to Marske and then back along the dunes.

Whitby East Cliff and St Mary's church from West Quay.

Large tracts of the Yorkshire coastline are very accessible. Much of it is in the care of the National Trust and a large section is contained within the boundary of the North York Moors National Park, which was created in 1952. In 1974 the Countryside Commission declared much of the area as a Heritage Coast and this helped stimulate interest in the region. A 36-mile section between Saltburn and Scalby Ness, just north of Scarborough, was defined as the North Yorkshire and Cleveland Heritage Coast.

In 1969, after nearly sixteen years of hard work securing access and improving the condition of the route, The Cleveland Way opened as a National Trail. The idea had first been conceived in 1930 by the Middlesbrough Rambling Club and today the Way presents an epic 108-mile adventure across the high North York Moors and some of the most spectacular sections of the Yorkshire Coast. The coastal section covers 45 miles of The Cleveland Way.

Much of the rest of the coastal route uses The Headland Way, a 20-mile route devised in 1993 which covers the very attractive section from Bridlington to link with The Cleveland Way at Filey Brigg.

The great thing about the Yorkshire Coast is that it can be undertaken as a single expedition, probably over seven to ten days, or a series of day trips. If you are undertaking the coastline as a single linear walk, I'd recommend a day's break from walking in both Scarborough and Whitby. Great public transport options, particularly coastal bus routes, make a linear day walk very easy to organise and if your preference is to walk the whole route as a holiday, there are plenty of places to stay within a reasonable day's walk of each other. There are a number of Sherpa-style baggage carrying services that will take your rucksacks or cases ahead of you to your night's accommodation, particularly on the Cleveland Way stretch.

The route is well covered by the Ordnance Survey maps and the Explorer 1:25000 scale maps are recommended as they provide a wealth of detail to ease navigation.

Chris Gee
York May 2016

Staithes and Roxby Beck from Cowbar Nab.

CHAPTER 1
BARMSTON TO BRIDLINGTON AND SEWERBY

Bridlington from the *Yorkshire Belle.*

Sewerby Rocks and South Cliff from North Sands, Bridlington.

Second World War pillbox, Highlands, Ulrome with Flamborough Head beyond.

Our Yorkshire Coast journey starts at Barmston, just south of Bridlington.

Although there are brief sections of coastal footpath on the Yorkshire Coast south of Bridlington, Fraisthorpe and Barmston, much of the boulder clay cliff top is devoid of rights of way and therefore the only options are to walk inland, sometimes on roads, or to work with the tide times and head along the beach.

While the boulder clay cliffs are fascinating and reveal fossils at low tide, the landscape is fairly uniform and there is a less of a sense of the spectacular between Barmston and Spurn Point, where Yorkshire ends by the mouth of the River Humber.

Barmston is a grand place to start this Yorkshire Coast adventure because it marks the beginning of a transition, from the boulder clay cliffs of Holderness, where the coast is constantly changing, to the dramatic chalk cliffs beyond Bridlington. It's also an excellent place from which to launch an arrival into Bridlington, a little bit of calm before the hustle and bustle of this busy seaside town.

There is parking here and it's accessible by the East Yorkshire Motor Services bus which plies the nearby A165 between Bridlington and Hornsea.

Barmston Sands looking to Flamborough Head.

The coastal walk starts in Barmston itself and the beach is easily accessible from the end of the no through road. An alternative is to follow inland Hamilton Hill Road – a chalky track by Hamilton Hill – through a landscape peppered with wartime pillboxes to join the beach at Fraisthorpe Sands. An alternative starting point is by Auburn Farm, a nice whitewashed single-storey farmstead close to the site of the medieval Auburn village. There is little to be seen of the

Auburn Farm near Fraisthorpe Sands.

village on the ground now and a close study of the Ordnance Survey map will reveal a number of abandoned medieval villages along this section of coast – Auburn, Wilsthorpe and Hilderthorpe.

These were all generally abandoned due to coastal erosion. There will have been more of course; Hartburn for example, was abandoned in the 15th century and Winkton in the mid-nineteenth century, but these have now disappeared from maps because in the last 600 years the coast has retreated and the North Sea has advanced.

Auburn Chapel was dismantled in the 1780s and any indication of a village on this site is now only revealed through aerial surveys or ground investigation. Hilderthorpe, closer to Bridlington, has fared much better and there are still some well-preserved earthwork remains which help with understanding the layout of this abandoned village. It is still possible to work out the position of houses, crofts and lanes. The neighbouring fields also clearly display evidence of the ridge and furrow method. Hilderthorpe has been listed as a Scheduled Ancient Monument. It was finally abandoned during the nineteenth century.

Bridlington South Sands looking to Flamborough Head.

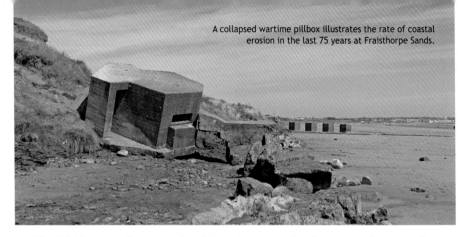
A collapsed wartime pillbox illustrates the rate of coastal erosion in the last 75 years at Fraisthorpe Sands.

The Holderness Coast south of Fraisthorpe is the fastest eroding coastline in Europe, at a rate of 5 feet per year. Every year, 2 million tonnes of coastline are lost to the sea. Winter storms gouge huge chunks of boulder clay from the cliffs, revealing new fossils, but this means maintaining cliff top rights of way is a huge challenge. Huge cracks can appear in the fields and grasslands above the cliffs and come the next season, the cliff face will have dropped away as the coastline advances west. For those of us who remember our geography lessons, Holderness is a classic example of longshore drift and a small portion of the eroded material is transported by the sea down to Spurn Point at the mouth of the Humber which continues to extend as a result of the material deposit from erosion further north.

Research suggests that the coastline was a further 3 miles east in Roman times. This particular coastline is so susceptible to erosion, because there is little to protect it. The long north-easterly fetch brings strong currents and powerful waves to attack the soft boulder clay which offers little resistance. The boulder clay itself is a reminder that Holderness was once a coastal bay that silted up during the last ice age. This is why it reveals fossils from time to time when the cliffs collapse.

Devil's toenails, are the most common fossil revealed, although ammonites, belemnites and crinoids are also reasonably common. Devil's toenails are the common name for Gryphaea, a kind of extinct bivalve oyster and they are particularly common along the entire length of the Yorkshire Coast. These oysters would once have lived on the sea bed of shallow waters and the fossils you find today typically date back to the Triassic and Jurassic period, roughly 150-200 million years ago. Tradition has it that carrying one with you will help you avoid rheumatism! One will be enough; they are certainly not lightweight...

Fossils: Two Gryphaea ('Devil's Toenails'), a belemnite and an ammonite, Barmston.

Barmston is also a good place to start because it is just about at sea level and marks one of the lowest points on the Yorkshire Coast. Our journey north to the highest point on Boulby Cliffs north of Staithes is generally uphill. The low lying land here was identified by military planners as high risk for a point of invasion and evidence of the defences installed during the Second World War to protect our coastline is still very visible today.

Pillboxes can be found on the beach and at the rear of the beach, another measure of how much our coastline has changed since the early 1940s. Coastal erosion has taken its toll and now some of these pillboxes have collapsed as they have been undermined by the tide. A row of concrete tank traps lines the dunes, designed to hold up advancing military vehicles that may have landed on the broad beach from enemy landing craft. Most pillboxes are of the Northern Command 'Lozenge' type and were built in 1940 and into early 1941.

The landscape behind the beach is dunes with marram grass, a rare example on this stretch of Yorkshire Coast. The only other place where we will briefly come across a dune system is at Cattersty Sands north of Skinningrove.

The best approach to Bridlington is at low tide and to stride out across South Sands. Passing Hilderthorpe and the Spa Theatre, we quickly arrive at Bridlington Harbour. There has been a theatre on this site since 1896, but the current Spa Theatre was opened on 29 July 1932, a popular dancing and concert hall. Fully refurbished and reopened in 2008, the Spa is still a popular concert theatre.

Below: Fraisthorpe Sands wartime tank traps illustrate how vulnerable to invasion this section of the Yorkshire Coast was.
Right: Fraisthorpe Sands: an old wartime pillbox sits helpless on the beach, at the mercy of the tides.

Bridlington Harbour is still one of Yorkshire's busiest fishing ports.

Bridlington Harbour is a busy port. North Pier and South Pier shelter a mix of fishing boats and leisure craft and the harbour is also the home of the *Yorkshire Belle*. The *Yorkshire Belle* was purpose-built in 1947 by shipbuilders Cook, Welton and Gemmell in Beverley, for pleasure trips from Bridlington Harbour, joining a fleet of six pleasure craft that operated boat trips out into Bridlington Bay. She was built as a replacement for the previous *Yorkshire Belle* which struck a mine in the River Humber during the Second World War and was lost with all hands.

The *Yorkshire Belle* continues in its role as a pleasure cruiser, offering trips along the spectacular coast from Bridlington Harbour, around Flamborough Head to Bempton Cliffs. Along with brief excursions, the *Yorkshire Belle* in conjunction with the Royal Society for the Protection of Birds (RSPB) offers morning and afternoon excursions to see the spectacular sea birds nesting on the cliffs around Flamborough and Bempton. The harbour is also popular with those who want to try their hand at sea fishing and day trips are available. The huge stone piers that protect the harbour are popular with day-trippers taking in the air, munching on their fish and chips. The calls of herring gulls, that classic seaside soundtrack, are ever present. If you look closely, Turnstones can be seen scurrying along the stone piers, seeking titbits and scraps left by the trawlermen around the working harbour. There are still cannon positioned on the stone piers, though they are ornamental these days.

Bridlington Harbour is also home to the *Yorkshire Belle*.

Bridlington Harbour and a fishing boat undergoes a repaint and maintenance.

High Street, Bridlington Old Town.   Bayle gatehouse, Kirkgate, Bridlington Old Town.

Bridlington is a classic seaside resort, all amusement arcades, rides for children, candy floss, fish and chips, shellfish stalls and hustle and bustle. It's still a popular day trip destination for families from South and West Yorkshire, much as it always has been since the railways first made that trip possible back in 1846. The York and North Midland Railway opened their station in Bridlington on 6 October 1846. At first it was the terminus of the new line from Hull, but a year later the line was extended on to Filey and Scarborough and remains in use today. The station is worth a visit, it's a Grade II listed building and has won heritage awards for its restoration. The staff and volunteers take pride in their floral displays and the station buffet is one of the few original railway station buffets surviving.

The Old Town is also worth seeking out, with highlights including the impressive priory gatehouse and the delightful old High Street and Westgate. There is an excellent Town Trail to be found online. Bridlington's Augustinian Priory in Kirkgate was established in 1113 and became one of the wealthiest in all Yorkshire. It was a popular place of pilgrimage and notable visitors included King Henry V in 1415. The dissolution that came with the Reformation in 1537 led to the demolition of much of the original priory and only the nave survives. The priory gatehouse – The Bayle – also survives and today houses the Bayle Museum. Built in 1388, the gatehouse survived demolition during the Dissolution of the Monasteries as by then it was in use as a courthouse and over the intervening centuries has been used as a prison, a school, a garrison and briefly as a town hall.

The Old Town was originally the heart of Bridlington, but as the harbour developed, the focus of the town shifted towards the quay. Some of the houses in the Old Town have early seventeenth-century origins, but much of the character of High Street and Westgate is Georgian.

Bridlington from the North Pier.

Bridlington North Pier during a winter storm.

BridlingtonPromenade – The Royal Prince's Parade.

Our route follows the promenade away from the harbour and runs parallel to North Sands. This is a glorious stretch as you stride out towards Sewerby. The hustle and bustle of the harbour area is quickly left behind and the view towards the towering white chalk cliffs of Sewerby and South Cliff on Flamborough Head tempt the walker away from Bridlington.

It is at Sewerby that these chalk cliffs dive down beneath the sands to be replaced by boulder clay on the journey south. The chalk is still there, deep below ground, resurfacing briefly in the Lincolnshire Wolds before heading on south below London to the South Downs and the chalk cliffs of Kent, Sussex and Dorset.

Bridlington marks the start of The Headland Way. This is a 20-mile long distance path that connects Bridlington with Filey and then links up with The Cleveland Way and Yorkshire Wolds Way at Filey Brigg. First devised in the early 1990s, The Headland Way technically starts at the Priory Church of St Mary in the Old Town in Bridlington. We stay with The Headland Way now all the way to Filey.

Our route climbs steadily from Bridlington to Sewerby Hall. Sewerby Hall is an elegant Georgian country house, built in 1714 for the Greame family. It is set in 50 acres of landscaped grounds next to the attractive village of Sewerby. The house was sold to Bridlington Corporation in 1934 and opened to the public on 1 June 1936. A £2.6 million restoration project which took two years to complete opened in August 2014. Sewerby is home to the Museum of East Yorkshire and the Coastguard Museum. The walled gardens and flower gardens are particularly well maintained and the grounds incorporate a small zoo.

The cricket ground and greens around Sewerby Hall offer a superb vantage point to look back across the sweep of Bridlington Bay. There is no shortage of benches here to take a break and enjoy the view!

Sewerby Hall.

Bridlington and North Sands from Sewerby.

Beyond Sewerby the route delivers our first encounter with the impressive Danes Dyke. The Dyke is spectacular on any scale. First impressions are of a deep geological scar running across Flamborough Head peninsula and separating the headland from the mainland. But Danes Dyke was man made and when you are in it, you cannot fail to be impressed by the scale of human effort that must have been required to excavate this dramatic feature, long before the development of quality hand tools. The Dyke stretches almost 2 miles across Flamborough Head and is thought to have been a defensive structure.

Archaeologists have struggled to date its construction, some hypotheses suggest post Roman, but Bronze Age arrowheads found during excavations have prompted archaeologists to think again. Current thinking is that it dates to the middle to late Bronze Age, common to other defensive and boundary earthworks found across the chalk hills of the Yorkshire Wolds. It is almost certainly nothing to do with Danes, a name that was probably attached to the Dyke much later in history, though the area east of Danes Dyke is still referred to as Little Denmark, thanks largely to a Danish settlement that came much later in about 800AD. Danes Dyke consists of both a bank and a ditch, the bank being constructed from material excavated from the ditch. The Dyke is a Scheduled Ancient Monument of national importance.

Danes Dyke is now a Local Nature Reserve as woodland has colonised the deep ditch. There are exotic species too, a legacy of the time when the Dyke was part of the estate of the Lady of the Manor of Flamborough. Ash, elm, lime, beech and sycamore have recolonized the ditch. Before the trees develop their leaves, the woods put on a display of snowdrops, winter aconites and bluebells.

Left: Dykes End, the southern end of Danes Dyke illustrating the depth to which Bronze Age tribes managed to excavate.

Below: Danes Dyke from the *Yorkshire Belle*.

SUGGESTED SHORT WALKS

Wartime pillbox, Barmston Sands, looks out to distant Bridlington.

Fraisthorpe Sands and nesting sandmartins recently arrived from Africa.

Barmston and Fraisthorpe Sands   (4 miles / 6.6km)

This is a low level walk which enjoys grand seaward views across to Flamborough Head and some of the rolling countryside of Holderness just inland from the coast. The low-lying land was vulnerable during wartime and the countryside is dotted with Second World War pillboxes.

Spring is a good time to visit when the arable fields will be host to the delightful calls of skylarks, yellowhammers and meadow pipits. It's possible to see kingfishers, dragonflies and damselflies on Barmston Drain. Sandmartins will be nesting in holes in the soft boulder clay cliffs.

The walk starts in Barmston and the church is worth a visit. All Saints church is a Grade I listed building.

Head north from the main street in Barmston along Hamilton Hill Road. This is a stony track that winds through delightful countryside with excellent views out to sea. It gains a little height as it skirts Hamilton Hill. In the fields between the hill and the coast, a number of wartime pillboxes can be seen.

The path continues north beyond Hamilton Hill to meet with the end of Sands Road. Keep ahead on the path to The Earl's Dike and turn right to follow this delightful waterway to where it outfalls onto the beach. The arrival on Fraisthorpe Sands reveals the broad sweep of beach that heads north to Bridlington and there are views beyond to the gleaming white chalk cliffs of Flamborough Head. The best option, if the tide is out, is to head south along the beach to Barmston Sands and Barmston Main Drain where it is possible to climb back off the beach and join the footpath that winds along South Field Lane back into Barmston.

Sewerby and Danes Dyke   (4 ½ miles / 7.2 km)

This walk offers an introduction to the chalk cliffs beyond Bridlington, a visit to a Bronze Age defensive earthwork and eighteenth-century Sewerby Hall. There are extensive views back to Bridlington and easy access to the shore for closer inspection of the chalk cliffs and the opportunity to indulge in some rock pooling. There are a few ups and downs on the coastal section.

The walk starts by The Ship Inn in Sewerby village and a path between fences leads out to the clifftop. The sweep of Bridlington Bay to the west is the first dramatic view of the walk. North Sands dominate the scene. The route turns left along the grassy path on the clifftop above Sewerby Rocks and heads directly for Danes Dyke.

The path drops down into the wooded Danes Dyke at Dykes End. This is a fascinating glimpse into this huge defensive structure stretching nearly 2 miles across Flamborough Head to the other Dykes End near Bempton. A chance to reflect on the mammoth undertaking this would have been for the Bronze Age tribes that would have relied on only basic tools nearly 4000 years ago.

Below: Sewerby Clock Tower tea room.
Right: Sewerby Hall Gardens: this is the walled garden.

Dykes End near Sewerby looking towards distant Bridlington.

The route climbs back up the other side of the Dyke and on up to Beacon Hill, passing one of several Second World War pillboxes that line the East Riding coast. It looks set to topple into the sea one day as cliff falls have gradually started to undermine its position.

Our path turns inland on Beacon Hill, the highest point of today's walk, where we are rewarded for the climb with a grand view across Flamborough Head to its two lighthouses.

Our route heads along a fence to Beacon Farm and Flamborough village. Flamborough village is worth a brief exploration to seek out Flamborough Castle, the remains of a chalk-built tower which is more likely to have been a fortified medieval manor house.

Exit from Flamborough is via Water Lane near the cemetery and a footpath strikes out between wire fences and across a field and animal enclosures to a belt of trees and the lane to Home Farm. The route heads on back down into Danes Dyke near the car park, crosses a bridge and then climbs back up again, signposted to Sewerby village. The footpath continues west in a straight line past Bridlington Links golf course with sea views now on offer again and past Danes Dyke Farm to pass another wartime pillbox and emerge on the cricket field at Sewerby Hall, which if it is open is well worth a visit. Ahead lies The Ship Inn and the start of the walk.

Above: Flock of sanderling, Sewerby Rocks.
Right: Oystercatchers, Sewerby Rocks.

Sunset over Bridlington and North Sands from Sewerby.

Sewerby Rocks and chalk boulders scattered on the beach, looking towards Bridlington.

CHAPTER 2
FLAMBOROUGH HEAD

Selwicks Bay from Flamborough Head with thrift in bloom.

North Landing, seen from High Holme.

South Landing from West Nook.

We drop down into Danes Dyke and climb back out again immediately. The Headland Way climbs up to Beacon Hill – the first of several beacons we will encounter on this walk. In the days before modern communications, a chain of signal stations using fires to transmit messages from high ground to high ground was the fastest way of sending messages up and down country, far quicker than a man on horseback could achieve. The principle reason would be to raise the alarm should enemy ships be sighted. As we walk along this clifftop path, Second World War pillboxes will be a reminder that the threat of invasion from the sea has only receded in recent times.

While our route heads along the top of the chalk cliffs, at low tide it is possible to walk the chalk shoreline across Sewerby Rocks. This is a grand place for rock pooling and in winter is home to flocks of oystercatcher, sanderling, turnstone and redshank. It's a great place to study the chalk cliffs in detail. Chalk is really effective at reflecting the light and even on a hot summer's day, the chalk will be very cool to the touch.

South Landing with its inshore lifeboat station, seen from East Nook.

The coastal path continues down into South Landing, past the lifeboat station and then back up again onto South Cliff. The lifeboat station, operated by the Royal National Lifeboat Institution (RNLI) for 135 years, continues to maintain an inshore lifeboat. 540 lives have been saved in its history.

Two lighthouses now come into view. The more modern and typical lighthouse is painted brilliant white and sits on Flamborough Head. It was built in 1806 and first lit on 1 December of that year. In common with all lighthouses around the British Isles, automation was to come and May 1996 saw the last lighthouse keepers depart. The lighthouse is still owned and operated by Trinity House. The older, angular tower further inland is the oldest surviving complete lighthouse in England. It was built in 1674 and a brush fire was originally intended to have been lit on the flat platform on the top. However, it was never lit; perhaps the strong winds would have blown the brushwood straight off any flat platform! Today the chalk-built lighthouse sits on the edge of the golf course and is a Grade II-listed building.

The modern day coastguard station which replaced a series of much smaller lookouts along the coastline is located nearby.

As we round Flamborough Head we meet the more modern lighthouse. Below is the fog station, still active today and a measure of how treacherous this section of coast can still be for shipping. Flamborough Head was until recent times used regularly for practice exercises by the RAF Air Sea Rescue teams in their Sea King helicopters, soon to be retired from active service after forty-seven years of operational duty.

Left: Flamborough Head's 1806-built lighthouse.
Below: The old 1674-built lighthouse, Flamborough Head.
Inset: An RAF Sea King rescue helicopter undertakes an exercise at Flamborough Head.

Selwicks Bay from Flamborough Head lighthouse.

Flamborough Head juts markedly out from the Yorkshire Coast into the North Sea, extending a good 6 miles out from the mainland. It can often be clear of cloud and sunny when inland clouds are building. It is also the first landfall for many migrant birds when making the journey across from the south and the east. Filey Brigg, which we will encounter further north, offers similar early landfall for migrating birds. In late spring and summer, sandmartins can be seen zipping to and from their nests in the soft earth that fringes the top of the chalk cliffs.

The view from the coastal path between the fog station and lighthouse is stunning, particularly looking across Selwicks Bay to Stottle Bank Nook. The section from here to Bempton Cliffs is one of the highlights of the Yorkshire Coast path and so early in the journey too! Early morning or late summer evening is the best when the rising and setting sun lights the chalk cliffs spectacularly. At lower tides, the scores of deep cut caves under the chalk cliffs are immediately apparent. The rise and fall of the tides can completely cover and reveal these brooding caves in a brief moment if the sea is on a heavy swell. Selwicks Bay is popular with families and it's a great place to explore the rock pools and caves. You might find yourself being watched by a grey seal spy-hopping out in the bay.

Flamborough Head is famous (mostly in the United States) for the naval battle that took place on 23 September 1779 between a small fleet under the command of American John Paul Jones and two Royal Navy vessels who were escorting a merchant convoy. The Battle of Flamborough Head has taken on a kind of iconic status as one of the principal naval actions of the American War of Independence, although the details of what actually happened are sketchy. Accounts from both sides are radically different, but it is acknowledged that having lost his own ship – the *Bonhomme Richard* – Jones captured the British *Serapis* and escaped in her.

Flamborough Head lighthouse from offshore.

The coastal path continues beyond Selwicks Bay, passing more wartime pill-boxes and on to the section between Stottle Bank Nook and North Landing. This is a wonderful stretch and a visit should be timed for late May or June to enjoy the natural spectacle. The chalk cliffs around Cradle Head, Breil Head, Breil Nook and Carter Lane are home to a large seabird colony. The onomatopoeic call of kittiwakes is an easy identifier for these endangered gulls. Fulmars, a relative of the albatross, will be riding the updrafts; these are skilled flying birds, able to fly great distances with seemingly little effort. And then there are the auks – guillemots, razorbills and everybody's favourite, puffins. The Yorkshire Wildlife Trust manages this section of the coast – Flamborough Cliffs Nature Reserve – and it is one of the best places in the country to see puffins on mainland Britain. Early morning or late summer evening is again best when the light seeks out the chalk cliffs. It might also be possible to see gannets just offshore heading to and from their colony at nearby Bempton.

Complementing the seabird spectacle in spring and summer is a colourful array of wildflowers on the clifftops. Thrift, red campion, ox eye daises, bird's foot trefoil and early purple orchids are amongst the colourful highlights of a varied selection of coastal plants that will delight the botanist. Meadow pipits flit around the meadows up here and the burbling call of skylarks is ever present. Be on the lookout for kestrels which hunt the small mammals and birds on these cliff top fringes.

Below: Selwicks Bay, the fog signal station and Flamborough Head light-house, all seen from Stottle Bank Nook.

Far left: Puffins at the Yorkshire Wildlife Trust's Flamborough Cliffs Nature Reserve.

Left: A meadow pipit amongst the red campion at Flamborough Cliffs Nature Reserve.

Above: Thornwick Bay and Thornwick Nab from High Holme. Beyond are Bempton Cliffs and Filey Bay.

Inset: Traditional Yorkshire cobles hauled out at North Landing.

The route soon arrives in North Landing, a hidden gem of a cove and another spectacular point to view the dramatic chalk cliff scenery. Rusting tractors haul traditional Yorkshire cobles in from the surf onto the beach and up onto the slipway. These are generally used for crab and lobster fishing, but also offer tourist trips around the headland. Yorkshire cobles are said to have their origins in Viking long ships. They are broad in the middle section (amidships) and high at both the bow and stern, not dissimilar to the Viking long ship image we are all familiar with. This design offers stability, as well as being easy to beach and the high bow allows them to cut through choppy waves and surf. The *Yorkshire Belle* might also be passing on its way from Bridlington to Bempton on a Seabird Cruise.

The Headland Way continues on around High Holme and Thornwick Bay, past Thornwick Nab on to North Cliff. From Sewerby to North Cliff there are ample cafés at which to stock up on provisions, at Flamborough Head itself, North Landing and Thornwick Nab. All offer parking facilities.

Beyond North Cliff we climb up onto Noon Nook for a spectacular view back to the whole of Flamborough Head, watched over by a tall wooden puffin. We pass Dykes End, the northern end of the deep Danes Dyke and beyond lies Bempton Cliffs and another wildlife experience.

SUGGESTED SHORT WALK

Flamborough Head (7 miles / 11.3 km)

This is a spectacular walk to see the best of the chalk cliff scenery around Flamborough Head and if undertaken in spring the opportunity to see a wildlife spectacle too at the Yorkshire Wildlife Trust's Flamborough Cliffs Nature Reserve.

The walk starts at South Landing, south of Flamborough village. There is a car park here. Head down the lane to the lifeboat station at South Landing and if the tide is out, this is a good opportunity to explore the rocky foreshore and to enjoy some rock pooling. Chalk boulders litter the shoreline.

Our route starts with an energetic climb along the coastal path up steps to East Nook. We then follow a breezy clifftop path along South Cliff with excellent views north across the headland to the two lighthouses, gleaming white. The path continues across New Fall and Old Fall – the Ordnance Survey leaving us a clue that the cliffs here are fragile and rock falls are not uncommon.

The route makes a spectacular arrival at Flamborough Head as it rounds the headland by High Stacks, a partly separated chunk of chalk cliff which will inevitably become an island in centuries to come.

Below: Flamborough Lighthouse across fields of oilseed rape from Old Fall.

Right: High Stacks seen from the shore at Cattlemere Scar.

The path continues to the fog signal station and then heads west to the newer lighthouse. This is a splendid place to pause and admire the view across Selwicks Bay to Stottle Bank Nook.

The onward route continues past the pub, shop and public toilets and heads for the beacon by the lane to the car park. Steps lead down towards Selwicks Bay, but then climb back up again through gorse, passing a wartime pillbox.

The coastal path continues between the cliffs of Stottle Bank Nook and the golf course and it is worth pausing here to look back at the old seventeenth-century lighthouse that never got to light its flame.

From Stottle Bank the clifftop path heads through wildflower meadows above a number of coves and inlets, by Cradle Head and Breil Head to Breil Nook. Between April and July these chalk cliffs will be a cacophony of sound as tens of thousands of nesting seabirds make these sheer cliffs their home and get down to the serious business of breeding and raising chicks.

Puffins, guillemots, razorbills, kittiwakes, fulmars and shags are all common along this stretch of the coast. Peer over the edge and they will be seen rafting on the surface of the sea below as well as clinging to the cliffs on impossibly thin ledges. Location is everything and the earliest arrivals will have bagged the best spots.

Left: A pair of nesting Razorbills on Breil Head at the Yorkshire Wildlife Trust's Flamborough Cliffs Nature Reserve.

Below: Breil Nook from Cradle Head.

Flowering thrift on East Scar near North Landing.

In spring the clifftop paths will be a riot of colour as coastal flowers bloom and the buzz of insects will never be far away.

The route winds round into North Landing where there is a café, toilets and car park. Some fishing boats may well be hauled up on the slipway below.

The coastal path then heads on past the car park, out to High Holme and round to Thornwick Bay. The winding path, inlets and coves offer ever changing views of the cliffs and the sea caves below. There is something especially appealing on a sunny day of the combination of blue sky, green grass, white chalk and blue sea.

As you approach the lane to the car park and café at Thornwick Bay, cross the track, follow the footpath to Thornwick Farm and then head through the caravan site to North Marine Road.

To finish, turn right along North Marine Road into Flamborough village and return to South Landing along South Sea Road to the starting point.

Below: High Holme from Thornwick Bay.

Right: Yorkshire coble *Summer Rose* laying crab and lobster pots off Flamborough.

Thornwick Nab from Thornwick Bay.

Thornwick Nab from North Cliff.

Flamborough Cliffs from the *Yorkshire Belle*.

CHAPTER 3

BEMPTON TO FILEY

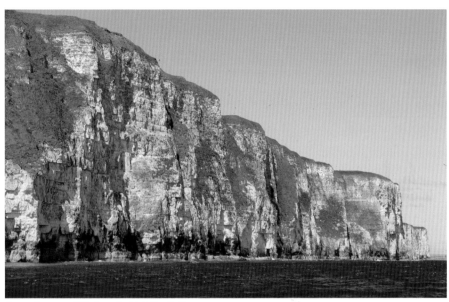

Above: Bempton Cliffs from the *Yorkshire Belle*.

Below: A gannet pair nesting at the RSPB Bempton Cliffs Reserve.

Puffins on the chalk cliff face at the RSPB's Bempton Cliffs Reserve

Bempton Cliffs offer another seabird spectacular along with some dramatic geological features. The sheer chalk cliffs here rival those on the south coast of England and the rock arch at Scale Nab is an impressive natural wonder. The geological upheavals that have happened here millions of years ago are clearly visible from the boat trips that ply the waters below the cliffs. In places, huge creases have been created in the rock face where the movement of tectonic plates has induced incredible forces on the cliff faces.

Bempton Cliffs is managed by the Royal Society for the Protection of Birds (RSPB) and there is a new visitor centre here. Bempton Cliffs is home to the largest gannet colony in mainland England. These are stunningly beautiful birds which can be found here all year round. They are amongst our largest seabirds, the adults an attractive brilliant white with exquisitely detailed black and grey beaks and a striking blue ringed eye.

All the other seabirds that make up the usual suspects can be found here too: guillemots, kittiwakes, fulmars, puffins, razorbills and gulls. In all, up to

A gannet comes in to land at the RSPB's Bempton Cliffs Reserve.

250,000 seabirds nest on the sheer cliffs between April and July. Viewing platforms are strategically placed at intervals to offer great views of these nesting seabirds. A visit in May and June is best. Come in December and the cliffs will be eerily quiet.

The gannets put on an impressive breeding display, gathering nesting material and with displays of mutual affection between partners, they are popular with photographers and birders.

In times past, not everyone who came to see the birds had good intentions. For centuries, local villagers would be lowered over the cliffs on ropes to harvest seabird eggs. Known as 'climmers', this practice was outlawed in 1869 with the passing of the Bird Protection Act. Egg collecting became illegal completely in 1954 and this has helped Bempton become the wildlife spectacle it is today.

Beyond Bempton lie the disused brick buildings of an old RAF radar station, another stark reminder of the role the East Coast played in facing off the threat of invasion from mainland Europe in the 1940s. The radar station closed in 1972.

The Headland Way continues on above the chalk cliffs past more intriguing names for the geological features – Mazey Shelves, Old Roll-up, New Roll-up, Crab Rocks, Bartlett Nab and Nettle Trip.

We reach a high point on Buckton Cliffs at the trig point, 135 metres above sea level and a grand view opens out of sheltered Filey Bay sweeping round to the protective arm of Filey Brigg.

Left: Scale Nab, the most impressive natural rock arch on the Yorkshire Coast, seen from the *Yorkshire Belle*.

Below: Buckton Cliffs looking down to Speeton Sands and Filey Bay; the trig point marks the end of the chalk cliffs and the beginning of boulder clay once again.

Buckton Cliffs from Speeton Sands.

Beyond this point, the chalk cliffs drop away completely at Speeton Cliffs and this is the last chalk we will see on our journey north to Saltburn. This is an important point on our geological journey as in the space of a few short miles we will pass from the chalk cliffs of the Cretaceous era to the Jurassic rocks and shales that start at Filey Brigg. The Jurassic era stretched from between 145 and 200 million years ago. The Cretaceous period is younger, from between 66 and 145 million years ago. The chalk cliffs are made up of the compressed calcite shells of deep sea marine organisms. Chalk is particularly porous and formed in layers which are distinctly visible on the sea cliffs when viewed from the water.

The Headland Way heads inland at Speeton Cliffs, passing the attractive chalk cobble church of St Leonard's before heading across fields to Reighton and then on into Filey. A more appealing option is to take the permissive path down through the scrub from Speeton Cliffs and onto Speeton Sands. It is essential to time this section with low tide for the easy stride along the sands to Filey.

Speeton Sands offers a last chance to look back to the towering chalk cliffs towards Buckton and Bempton before we set our sights on genteel Edwardian Filey.

The route passes Reighton Gap, on across Reighton Sands, past Hunmanby Gap and on to Hunmanby Sands and Muston Sands.

Along the way, if the tide is out, we see the rusting boiler of *Laura*, an Austrian schooner-rigged steamer, wrecked on 21 November 1897. There is more evidence of wartime defences here with crumbled tank traps and pillboxes on the beach.

Before long the route crosses Filey Sands and arrives on the promenade at Filey next to the paddling pool.

The boiler of the wrecked steamer *Laura*, Speeton Sands.

SUGGESTED SHORT WALKS

Bempton, Danes Dyke and North Cliff (3 ¼ miles / 5.2 km)

This is a walk that takes in the spectacular seabird colony at the RSPB Bempton Reserve, enjoys dramatic views of some impressive geological features and sweeping views to Flamborough Head. May to June is a good time to visit to enjoy the peak breeding season of the birds and the display of coastal flowers on the clifftops.

The walk starts at the RSPB's car park and visitor centre. There is a railway station at nearby Bempton and a bus service too.

Continue through or around the visitor centre and follow the footpath across grass to the coastal path above Crab Rocks. We join The Cleveland Way here and turn right, heading east. As soon as we reach the clifftop, the sound, smell and sight of the tens of thousands of seabirds assault the senses. In high season the cliffs are thronged with puffins, kittiwakes, guillemots, razorbills, fulmars and shags. You might have to search hard for a puffin, but they will be there and as we head further along the cliff to some of the quieter stretches of coastal path, you might well spot them here too.

Bempton is famous for its gannets and these huge white birds will be flying to and from their nest sites on the top of the cliffs, huge, strong wing beats carrying them on. When they land there is usually a bit of commotion while all the birds adjust to their own personal space and some tender greetings pass between pairs. When the red campion is in flower, the views of these bright white birds, against a blue backdrop, behind a fringe of pink blooms, is stunning.

Bempton Cliffs and Filey Bay seen from above Scale Nab.
Inset: A pair of courting gannets at the RSPB's Bempton Cliffs Reserve.

The rock arch of Scale Nab from Wandale Nab.

The coastal path continues past wooden viewing platforms at New Roll-up and Old Roll-up and before long the impressive rock arch of Scale Nab comes into view. There are few sea arches on the Yorkshire Coast and this is one of the most spectacular. The gannets have colonised it too and there will be scores of nesting birds on its upper slopes.

The Cleveland Way continues east past Wandale Nab and leaves the reserve and most of the birders behind. The path winds gently on to reveal grand views back to Filey Bay and Filey Brigg. Before long the path crosses Dykes End, the northern end of this Bronze Age defensive earthwork. As you head on past Dykes End and look inland, the embankment that forms part of the structure is clear to see, an impressive achievement indeed for those that built it, perhaps some 4000 years ago.

The walk then climbs up to Noon Nook and the wooden puffin that overlooks the fantastic view ahead to Flamborough Head. This is the high point of our walk and the turning point. The view reveals the various inlets and coves around Flamborough and the two lighthouses.

From here we retrace our outward route back to Bempton.

Dykes End and the northern end of Danes Dyke where the embanked earthwork is more apparent.

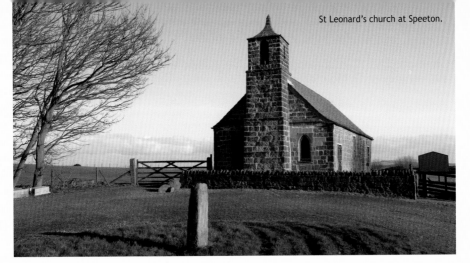
St Leonard's church at Speeton.

Speeton church and Buckton Cliff (3 ½ miles / 5.4 km)

This is a short walk to enjoy a lovely view of Filey Bay and to visit the tiny church of St Leonard's, a cobble-built church, built using local material. Speeton marks the end of the chalk cliffs.

It's possible to park in the small car park next to St Leonard's church. It's worth a brief look inside this church which dates to the early twelfth century. It is a very simple church standing alone in a field a little away from the village.

From the car park a footpath heads away, striking diagonally across fields towards Raikes Closes, passing old hedgerows. We drop down across the rippled landscape of Speeton Hills to arrive above Speeton Cliffs. To the left there is a permissive path down through scrub to Speeton Sands. A well-placed bench is a great place to sit and enjoy the spectacular view of Filey Bay with Filey clearly sheltered by the protective arm of the Brigg.

This is a place of transition, where the towering chalk cliffs of Bempton, Buckton and Speeton suddenly stop and the landscape changes dramatically back to boulder clay cliffs. The chalk has gone deep underground at this point.

Our route heads right towards the east on The Headland Way and climbs to the trig point on Buckton Cliffs, the highest point on this stretch, 135 metres above sea level and another great vantage point to admire the view back to Filey Bay. We turn around here and retrace the outward route back to Speeton church.

Filey Bay and Filey Brigg seen from Speeton Cliffs.

A wartime pillbox, now beached at Hunmanby Gap with Bempton Cliffs beyond.

The RNLI inshore lifeboat on exercise in Filey Bay.

Hunmanby Sands, Filey Bay and Filey Brigg from Hunmanby Gap.

CHAPTER 4

FILEY TO SCARBOROUGH

Filey seen from Filey Brigg.

Ornamental gardens, Filey looking to Filey Brigg.

Filey promenade.

Of all the Yorkshire coastal resorts, Filey is the one that has retained most period charm. It is essentially a Victorian and Edwardian resort, built in a naturally sheltered bay. The locals still put on an Edwardian Festival each year to celebrate the town's heyday. Filey is still a busy seaside resort today and evidently it is a very popular destination for ramblers.

No less than four long distance paths converge on Filey. The Headland Way, our route, has taken 20 miles along the coastal cliffs from Bridlington. The Centenary Way threads 83 miles from York, mostly across the Howardian Hills and Yorkshire Wolds. The Yorkshire Wolds Way has followed a route across the chalk landscape of the Yorkshire Wolds for 79 miles from the Humber Estuary. The Cleveland Way starts its journey in Helmsley, marches 108 miles across the North York Moors to the coast at Saltburn, before heading south along the coast to Filey. This latter long distance path will be our route to Saltburn.

These long distance routes would not have troubled the Walking Parson. Canon Arthur Neville Cooper was born in 1850 and was vicar of Filey for fifty-five years. He walked from Filey to London within a week, returning by train in time to catch his Sunday morning service. He's also credited with walking 741 miles to Rome in six weeks and 653 miles to Venice. Canon Cooper died aged ninety-three, proof positive that long distance walking can be good for your longevity. It's not recorded whether he completed the Yorkshire Coast.

Filey and coble landing seen from Filey Sands.

Filey was once home to Filey Holiday Camp. Opened in 1939 and operated by Butlins, such holiday camps have waxed and waned with the popularity of the seaside and Filey finally closed its doors in 1983. At its height, thousands of holidaymakers would be brought in on special trains to its own purpose-built railway station.

The town is worth exploring. Until the late eighteenth century, like most of the current resorts, Filey was just a large fishing village. However, the growth in popularity of Scarborough and Bridlington drove those seeking a quieter sanctuary away from the hustle and bustle to this attractive fishing village sheltered by the dramatic Filey Brigg. That attraction holds true today and generally Filey remains popular with those seeking a more restrained seaside experience.

From 1835, a Birmingham solicitor, John Wilkes Unett, bought 35 acres of land to the south of the old fishing village and began its development into a fashionable seaside resort. The elegant crescent that graces the clifftop above the gardens was built for Unett.

Filey railway station is a good option for exploring the Wolds Coast line between Hull and Scarborough and the train can be used to organise a number of linear coastal walks. The station retains its overall train shed designed by York and North Midland Railway architect G.T. Andrews. The station opened in 1846 when the line from Bridlington was extended to Scarborough. However, our coastal route continues along the promenade to coble landing where traditional Yorkshire fishing cobles are still hauled out on the slipway. The sands offer a fine vantage point to look back to Flamborough Head where the sun rises on a winter's morning.

A carved wooden fisherman illustrates the fishing heritage of this small resort, Filey promenade.

St Oswald's church, Filey.

It's worth a detour to the church of St Oswald or alternatively it is possible to climb through the gap in the cliffs near the sailing club to access the clifftops and Filey Country Park. St Oswald's church is a stout looking church with Norman origins. It was heavily rebuilt during the twelfth and thirteenth centuries.

From the country park it's well worth the optional detour onto Filey Brigg itself, a spectacular outcrop that also acts to shelter Filey Bay and the town. Filey Brigg can be the first landfall of migrating birds and therefore the Brigg and the bird hide below the cliffs on Spittal Rocks, looking out to Brigg End, are popular with birders.

Brigg End can be a turbulent point when the sea is rolling, but a good place to look out for seabirds, including shags. One of the earliest recorded shipwrecks in the country was at Filey Brigg. In 1542 a Scottish ship called *Martin* came to grief on Filey Brigg during a storm. The First World War saw German U-boats patrolling this section of the Yorkshire Coast, targeting British merchant ships. On 18 August 1917 a 1300 ton steamer *Ardens* was torpedoed just off Filey Brigg.

The Brigg offers the first dramatic view of the sweeping bay across to Scarborough with the castle dominating the view. The Brigg is here because it is formed of hard calcareous grit laid on top of Osmington Oolite which can be seen at low tide forming the slender finger that disappears below the waves. The softer boulder clay has borne the brunt of the elements and this continues to shift and collapse, but it is likely that the harder foundations of the Brigg will be here for some time to come.

Traditional Yorkshire cobles hauled out at Coble Landing, Filey.

Cunstone Nab seen across The Wyke from Newbiggin Cliff.

From Filey Brigg we rejoin the coastal walk. This is an exhilarating section, the day's destination almost always in sight. On our way we pass the old boundary between the East Riding of Yorkshire and the North Riding. The route follows The Cleveland Way across North Cliff, Newbiggin Cliff and on to Gristhorpe Cliff, passing one of the few caravan sites on the coastal walk.

Gristhorpe Cliff was the site of a spectacular rescue by the Filey Volunteer Life Saving Rocket Company. In March 1916, the HMS *Meking* came to grief on the shore. The volunteers fired their breeches buoy across the stricken vessel and managed to save the entire crew bar one.

Lebberston Cliff is a geological medley of Calcareous Grit, Oxford Clay, Boulder Clay, Sandstone and Limestone. The Red Cliff fault is responsible for thrusting this colourful combination into the limelight.

On rounding Lebberston Cliff the first reveal of Cayton Bay is a welcome sight. Cayton Bay is a popular beach and home to a developing surfing culture. It is also popular with families. The bay was clearly once a weak spot in Britain's defences and more wartime pillboxes line the sands. It's worth dropping down to the sands to explore the quieter reaches of the intriguingly named Johnny Flinton's Harbour. Whoever Johnny Flinton was remains a mystery.

Reaching out into the North Sea, Brigg End, Filey Brigg.

Gristhorpe Sands from Red Cliff Point.

Cayton Bay from Lebberston Cliff with Scarborough in the distance.

Cayton Bay is thought to be the source of the great stone monolith that can today be found in St Andrew's churchyard at Rudston, some 10 miles away. The Rudston Monolith was transported from Cayton Bay to Rudston over 3500 years ago and one can only marvel at the ingenuity that must have been employed at the time to move this 25 foot tall, 40 ton leviathan over that distance. It is the tallest megalith in the British Isles.

The route climbs steeply up from the beach through wooded Tenant's Cliff, up onto Osgodby Hill for a brief section through suburban Scarborough. Regaining the cliff top at Frank Cliff, on reaching Wheatcroft Cliff, a superb panorama opens out across South Bay. The view takes in the sweeping curve of the sands as they stretch from Holbeck Gardens and the Spa Complex to the castle on the headland.

Johnny Flinton's Harbour seen from Tenants Cliff wood.

SUGGESTED SHORT WALKS

North Cliff and Filey Brigg   (5 miles / 8 km)

The walk starts at The Crescent in Filey, an elegant sweeping Victorian terrace built between 1835 and 1850. From The Crescent, head into the park and past the bandstand to take the footpath that zig-zags down to the promenade. Head north along the promenade as far as Coble Landing where a small number of fishing boats are likely to be hauled up on the short slipway.

Just before Coble Landing, turn left along Church Ravine where the road runs through a deep, wooded cleft and climbs past the entrance to the country park to a roundabout. Take the Scarborough Road for ½ mile and turn right at Filey Field Farm onto a footpath that makes a beeline for the coast at Under Nine Rocks. An intriguing name: perhaps the Ordnance Survey lost count and just settled for less than nine and certainly not double figures!

Left: Filey Brigg from Coble Landing, Filey.

Below: Filey Brigg from Filey Country Park.

Arrival on the clifftop path is a revelation and the cliffs drop away steeply behind the low embankment. To the north and west are excellent views to Scarborough, dominated by its castle.

The route turns right along North Cliff and heads directly for Filey Brigg. It's well worth the expedition onto the exposed Brigg, with evidence of Roman occupation. This is where both The Yorkshire Wolds Way and Cleveland Way terminate, a place of pilgrimage for ramblers!

At low tide it is possible to descend paths to Old Quay Rocks and head out on a walkway to the end of the Brigg. Return to the landward end of the Brigg and head south along the grassy tops of North Cliff Country Park towards Filey town. Ahead is the low profile of St Oswald's church. At a deep ravine, the path drops down steps to the sailing club and deposits you on the beach and, if the tide permits, it's a short stroll along the beach to Coble Landing. Alternatively, climb back up the other side of the ravine to continue along the grassy cliff tops to steps above Church Ravine that take you down to Coble Landing and the promenade. Retrace the outward route here to the start.

Filey from Old Quay Rocks.

48

Lebberston Cliff and Cayton Bay from Cayton Cliff.

South Bay and Scarborough seen from Wheatcroft Cliff.

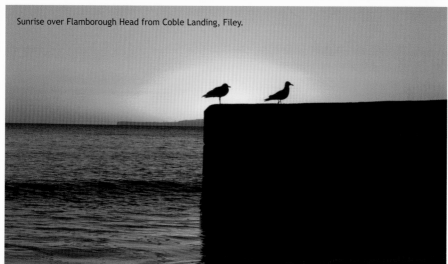

Sunrise over Flamborough Head from Coble Landing, Filey.

CHAPTER 5
SCARBOROUGH

Scarborough, its castle and headland seen from South Bay.

St Mary's church above Scarborough's old town and the old harbour.

Traditional seaside donkey rides, South Bay sands, Scarborough.

Scarborough is the spiritual home of the British seaside holiday. The discovery in 1620 of a so-called medicinal spring at the foot of South Cliffs kick-started a revolution and the popularity of spa holidays for recuperation of body and mind can be traced back to this point. Spa facilities were built and as the Victorians promoted the natural spring waters, the healing powers of sea water bathing and fresh air and exercise, the fortunes of Scarborough grew and grew.

South Bay is by far the most popular and on any given sunny summer day the beach will be busy with families. It's the only place on the Yorkshire Coast where you're likely to see donkeys still plying their trade on the beach.

It's worth taking some time to explore Scarborough on this section of the coastal walk. The approach from South Bay is a lovely way to arrive in the resort, the view ahead dominated by the castle on the headland that juts out and has given Scarborough protection from the elements that is the reason it is here today. Below the castle, the old town cascades down the hill, a jumble of houses and classic Yorkshire red pantiled roofs. These red pantile roofs are common across much of the North Riding of Yorkshire, but they originated in Holland. The red tiles were brought from the Netherlands as ships' ballast in empty boats returning to England, having sailed with export goods to Holland.

Scarborough Spa and The Grand Hotel, South Bay.

South Cliff Tramway, South Bay, Scarborough.

Central Tramway station, Scarborough.

The route passes Holbeck Gardens and South Cliff Gardens and soon arrives at the first of Scarborough's three cliff lifts. It's a mark of Scarborough's importance as a Victorian resort that it once had five of these funicular railways that quickly carried visitors from the top of the cliff to the promenade below, or perhaps more importantly, helped carry them to the top rather than negotiate the steep climb.

The two on North Bay have been dismantled, but the three on South Bay survive, two of which are in working order today.

The first you come across is the South Cliff Lift which links the gardens above South Cliff with the Spa Complex on the promenade. This was the first funicular railway to be built in Britain by the Scarborough South Cliff Tramway Company and was opened on the 6 July 1875. It was built by the Manchester engineering firm of Crossley Brothers, while Metropolitan Carriage & Wagon of Birmingham built the two cars, each accommodating 14 seated passengers. The system was operated by seawater pumped through a hydraulic system, filling a water tank on the upper car until the counterbalance point is reached, at which point the upper car began its descent with speed and safety controlled by a brakeman at the top station. Both cars were attached to the twin-steel cable rope and the weight of the descending car hauled the ascending car to the top.

The cars in use today were brought into service in 1935 by Hudswell Clarke & Company of Leeds. The railway is now operated by Scarborough Borough Council and the system was thoroughly overhauled in 1997 to become fully automatic.

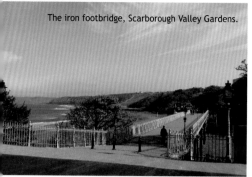

The iron footbridge, Scarborough Valley Gardens.

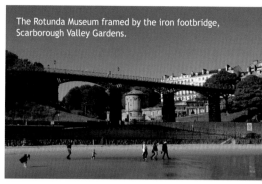

The Rotunda Museum framed by the iron footbridge, Scarborough Valley Gardens.

The Spa Gardens were laid out in the 1850s and in 1876 a new Spa Pavilion was built to replace the previous fire-damaged structure. The iron footbridge which spans the Valley Gardens was built in 1826 to make access easier.

The Rotunda Museum is a fascinating museum, purpose built in 1829 to house the collection of geologist William Smith. The building was designed to transport the visitor through geological time and a spiral staircase is used to great effect to display the collection in strict geological order. The museum was refurbished in 2008 and reopened as the William Smith Museum of Geology and houses a collection largely gathered from the Yorkshire and North East Coast.

We then pass the redundant St Nicholas Cliff Lift. This was a later addition to the seafront landscape and was built by the Medway Safety Lift Company, opening to the public on 5 August 1929. This was a broad gauge construction located on the south side of the Grand Hotel near the Aquarium. It closed in February 2007 as the cost of repairs to bring it up to modern standards was not affordable. It remains out of use, but intact and may be sold.

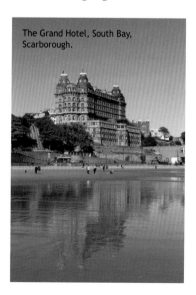

The Grand Hotel, South Bay, Scarborough.

Dominating the townscape above South Bay is The Grand Hotel, a fitting name for such a splendid building. It was built in 1867 to a design by architect Cuthbert Brodrick and at the time of its completion it was one of the largest hotels in the world. It is a Grade II-listed building and its design holds some remarkable secrets based around a theme of time. There are four corner towers which represent the four seasons; twelve floors, for each month of the year; 52 chimneys, for each week of the year and 365 rooms, to represent every day of the year. It is still a popular hotel today.

After passing The Grand Hotel we arrive at the third and final cliff lift, the Central Tramway. This funicular railway was built by the Central Tramway Company Scarborough Limited and opened to the public on 1 August 1881. Originally operated by a stationary steam engine, it was converted to electric power in 1910. The cars you see today date from 1932 and are driven remotely from the top station. The tramway has been fully restored and is still operational today.

The promenade then continues past amusement arcades and all the paraphernalia of a popular modern seaside resort to the lifeboat station.

Scarborough lifeboat station is one of the oldest in the country, opening in 1801. Sunderland and Montrose opened the year before. The current lifeboat station is being rebuilt to bring it up to modern standards.

The old harbour is worth exploring. It is still very much a working fishing harbour and plenty of fishing boats will be tied up if they are not out at sea. There has been a quay here since the thirteenth century and the central pier which dates to 1732 is a good place to buy fish; it doesn't come much fresher than this and for those that like shellfish, there are plenty of stalls selling cockles, mussels and whelks around the harbour.

The piers out to the east harbour are a popular location for day trippers to stroll and pleasure boat trips operate from the east pier out into South Bay.

Left: The RNLI's Scarborough lifeboat station.

Below: Scarborough east harbour with *Hatherleigh*, *Coronia* and *Regal Lady* at anchor.

The 1806 lighthouse on Vincent's Pier.

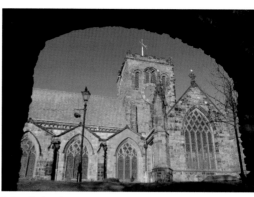

St Mary's church.

There is a lighthouse on Vincent's Pier which opened in 1806 and was fully automated in 1997.

Some fascinating old buildings still survive by the old harbour. The most interesting are to be found on Sandside, opposite the harbour. The medieval house known as King Richard's House dates back to Elizabethan times. Nearby is the old eighteenth-century Custom House and adjacent to the Newcastle Packet public house are the exposed timber frame remains of a thirteenth-century cruck house.

Strictly speaking The Cleveland Way and the coastal path follow the road around the headland from the old harbour to North Sands in North Bay. This is probably one for completists as the more appealing option is to climb up to the castle.

The best route is to head up to the church of St Mary, founded in the twelfth century. The remains of the old twelfth-century monastic church are still standing in the churchyard, though only the east wall survives. The replacement church dates largely from the seventeenth century and nineteenth century rebuilding.

The churchyard also contains the grave of Anne Brontë. Anne came to Scarborough regularly and it was on her last visit in May 1849 that she died of consumption (pulmonary tuberculosis), aged twenty-nine. She had been hoping that the fresh air and change of scene might stimulate a recovery after being ill with tuberculosis since December. Charlotte Brontë decided that Anne should rest where she had fallen and therefore Anne was buried at Scarborough, rather than Haworth where the rest of the family had been buried. Anne's grave is located in the small graveyard between the church and the castle approach. In 2011 a plaque commemorating Anne was laid by the Brontë Society in the churchyard.

Anne Brontë's grave.

Scarborough Castle keep was built during the reign of King Henry II between 1165 and 1168. The stout Norman keep presents a familiar silhouette to walkers on the coastal path and is visible at various stages from Flamborough Head to Hayburn Wyke. A Scots army supporting Cromwell's Parliamentarian troops laid siege to Scarborough during the English Civil War. The bombardment in 1645, possibly from Oliver's Mount, split the castle keep in two to create the outline we are familiar with today. The impressive curtain wall was built a little earlier in 1136 on the headland that has long acted as a natural strategic site for defending the two bays.

Scarborough Castle was at the centre of some of the heavy fighting of the English Civil War and changed hands several times between 1642 and 1649. After the Parliamentarian victory, Cromwell ordered the castle to be demolished like so many across the country. Legend has it that Scarborough Castle had been so badly damaged by such prolonged bombardment that no further demolition was required!

The First World War was not just fought on the Western Front in Northern France and Belgium; it came close to Scarborough too. On 6 June 1917 a 2300 ton merchant vessel, the *SNA II* was torpedoed by a German U-Boat and sank. On 24 August, the SS *Springhill* hit a mine off Scarborough and sank. Earlier in 1914 a German battlecruiser at anchor just off the coast of Scarborough fired its heavy guns on the town and considerable damage was caused. The eighteenth-century barracks within the curtain wall at the castle were destroyed during the bombardment. This must have been a very frightening experience for the Scarborough residents who had not had cause to feel threatened by war since 1779 when the American captain John Paul Jones had raided the town just before the famous Battle of Flamborough Head.

The Norman St Mary's Chapel, Scarborough Castle.

The Norman castle keep, Scarborough Castle.

Scarborough, the harbour and castle seen from Oliver's Mount.

The headland upon which Scarborough Castle was built has long had strategic advantage and the Romans built another of their coastal signal stations here as part of a chain of communication along the East Coast. The signal station was built in AD376, but by AD400 had been destroyed by Angle raiders.

There are also the remains of the Norman Chapel of Our Lady within the grounds of the castle.

The castle grounds provide excellent views of South Bay and the route taken from Filey. It also looks directly across at Oliver's Mount. Climbing Oliver's Mount is no small undertaking and so most people drive up in their cars, but it is worth the climb whichever way you tackle it for a bird's eye view of Scarborough which takes in much of the coastal route. It is apparently named Oliver's Mount because this is where Oliver Cromwell laid siege to Scarborough during the English Civil War, but there is scant evidence that Cromwell himself ever visited Scarborough. The most likely explanation is that Parliamentarian troops lined up their siege cannon on this high ground given its strategic advantage.

A special charter train, the Scarborough Spa Express, hauled by locomotive No.48151 departs Scarborough Station for York. The view is towards Burniston and Long Nab from Oliver's Mount.

An RAF Sea King helicopter displays during the annual Armed Forces Day event at Scarborough South Bay.

In June Scarborough hosts the Annual Armed Forces Day and Oliver's Mount is a good vantage point to watch the aerial displays which often include the Battle of Britain Memorial Flight and a Sea King helicopter.

Scarborough Fair, immortalised in that traditional folksong, was held annually for forty-five days from mid-August and attracted traders and shoppers from all over the country and even from Northern Europe. It was granted by King Henry III in 1253 and was held for over 500 years until 1788.

Scarborough is still very much a holiday resort and is a popular day trip destination. The railway still brings day trippers to Scarborough from Leeds and York and further afield and in summer it is a popular destination for steam hauled excursions, including the Scarborough Spa Express and the Scarborough Flyer.

From the castle the route drops down to North Sands and the promenade that leads round to Northstead Manor Gardens and on to the Oceanarium at Scalby Mills. Set back from South Bay is Peasholm Park, created in 1912 on an oriental theme. It is famous for the scale model battleships which entertain visitors with mock engagements during the school holidays. The North Bay Railway is a 20 inch gauge miniature railway opened in 1931 and operating over a mile of track between Peasholm Park and Scalby Mills. Four diesel locomotives with a steam outline have operated the line since the early 1930s, but in 2016, in a break with tradition, the volunteers at the railway have built their very own steam locomotive *Georgina* to operate some of the services.

The Oceanarium or Sea Life Centre at Scalby Mills is a giant aquarium with indoor and outdoor display areas for a close encounter with some of our aquatic life.

SUGGESTED SHORT WALKS

Scarborough Town Trail

This town trail is an excellent way to explore the historic hinterland around Scarborough's South Bay.

The walk starts by The Grand Hotel and then continues into St Nicholas Cliff, passing the location of The Cliff where Anne Brontë stayed before her death in 1849.

The Mount and South Cliff Gardens seen from South Bay sands.

Heading on into St Nicholas Street the route passes the Long Room and the Royal Hotel, some of the older hotels in Scarborough, as well as the upper station for the Central Tramway, the oldest cliff lift in the country.

The walk continues on past the Town Hall, formerly St Nicholas House. Theakston's Bookshop is on the left. At the crossroads turn left into Newborough and Newborough Bar is on the left. Crossing the road and turning right to head back towards the crossroads, our route heads left into St. Thomas Street where we find the Theatre Royal.

Scarborough North Bay seen from the castle walls.

Return once again to the crossroads and this time turn left into Newborough. Turn right into Blands Cliff for a close look at The Bell Hotel. Return once again

to the junction with Newborough and head straight across to the Market Hall. Continue around the northern side of the Market Hall into St Sepulchre Street to pass Trinity House on the right and the old Quaker Meeting House on the left.

Far left: The Elizabethan King Richard III House near the old harbour.

Left: The 1806 built lighthouse on Vincent's Pier.

Heading on along St Sepulchre Street and right into West Sandgate we pass the Butter Cross and across the way is The Bolts. Our route then heads down to Sandside where in quick succession we pass King Richard III House, the site of Scarborough's shipbuilding industry and the Three Mariners Inn. From the inn we double back left into Quay Street to locate the Long Greece Steps which take us steeply up into Castlegate. At the top turn left into Paradise to pass Paradise House and then take a right turn up Church Lane to visit Anne Brontë's grave.

From here there is the option to visit Scarborough Castle or return to Church Lane and St Mary's parish church and then down Church Street Stairs to visit John Wesley. From here you have the option of a direct descent to Foreshore Road for a right turn back to The Grand Hotel or turn right into Long Westgate to the junction with Queen Street which takes you back to Newborough and an alternative route to The Grand Hotel via St Nicholas Street.

Right: A harpoon gun, Vincent's Pier, Scarborough harbour.

Below: The lighthouse and pleasure craft *Coronia* seen from the castle.

Scarborough Castle Keep.

Scarborough old harbour.

CHAPTER 6
SCARBOROUGH TO RAVENSCAR

Scarborough Castle from Scalby Ness.

Sunrise over Scarborough Castle from Scalby Ness.

Cromer Point.

From Scalby Mills we quickly leave Scarborough behind and climb up onto Long Nab on Scalby Ness. This is a good point to look back and appraise the view across North Bay to Scarborough Castle. Ness is Viking for headland and the Vikings were responsible for naming much of the Yorkshire Coast.

We are then back on the coastal clifftop path and our route continues on to Cromer Point. Cromer Point is a great place to come and watch a winter sunrise behind Scarborough Castle and the view back towards the headland and North Bay is glorious. Cromer Point has clearly been a treacherous place for shipping in times past and some of the rock outcrops are named on maps as Sailor's Grave.

The coastal route continues on The Cleveland Way on a cliff top path that winds alongside fields by way of Crook Ness, Burniston Wyke, Long Nab, Creek Point and Hundale Point. The sedimentary rocks that make up this coastline were formed long ago when dinosaurs roamed the planet. Dinosaur footprints up to 2 feet across have been found on the shore at Burniston Wyke. There is a former coastguard lookout point at Long Nab which operated from 1927 until 1992. It is now used as a bird observatory to look for migrating birds. The coastal path turns east into Cloughton Wyke, the first of a number of Wykes on this stretch of coast-

line. Wyke is commonly used in this part of North East Yorkshire and is thought to have Norse origins for a place where a boat can be landed and there is access from the beach. Wick is Norse for bay so it is likely to be a corruption of that. Just before Cloughton Wyke is Hun Dale, one of the shortest of all Yorkshire's Dales – only about 430 yards long – but particularly attractive when the gorse is in bloom.

Cloughton Wyke from Hundale Point.

Hundale Point was the scene of a dramatic shipwreck in December 1894 when a 1230 ton steam schooner *Richmond* ran aground while heading from Rotterdam to Tyneside. The crew of the *Richmond* were all rescued by the local rocket brigade.

At low tide Hundale Scar reveals a rock pavement with clints and grikes just like those found on the limestone pavements of the Yorkshire Dales. Cloughton Wyke also reveals much evidence of coastal erosion; large cubes of rock have fallen from the cliff face to the shore leaving huge holes in the cliff face like some gap toothed grin in the mouth of the Wyke. Nesting kittiwakes can be found here on the cliffs around Salt Pans, a clue as to the former industry here.

Beyond Cloughton Wyke the coastal path continues its climb towards Ravenscar and heads into more wooded territory around Hayburn Wyke. It's worth the descent down onto the rocky beach in Hayburn Wyke to see the cascade where Hayburn Beck topples into the sea. The beach consists of massive boulders, cobbles and pebbles. The landscape around Hayburn Wyke is owned and managed by the National Trust, like so much of Yorkshire's coast. The woodland is particularly appealing in early spring when bluebells, wild garlic and wood sorrel carpet the woodland floor before the tree canopy has had time to block out the light. The path to the Wyke winds down through twisted and gnarled oak trees, like corkscrews reaching for the light.

Little Cliff from Hundale Scar.

Hayburn Wyke from Little Cliff.

Climbing steeply out of Hayburn Wyke on a lop-sided (but secure) wooden staircase, The Cleveland Way resumes its clifftop journey to Petard Point and along to the wooded cliffs of Beast Cliff. It's worth remembering to look back for excellent views towards Scarborough Castle and an appreciation of the height gained on the journey from Scalby Mills. Flamborough Head and Filey Brigg are also in sight on a clear day.

It's also worth a diversion inland to Cloughton Station. Closed in March 1965, the station is restored and is now a tea room and offers accommodation too.

Beyond Beast Cliff, the coastal clifftop path resumes its journey on to Common Cliff and above Blea Wyke to the rocket post on the approach to Ravenscar.

The route arrives in Ravenscar with a dramatic reveal of Robin Hood's Bay laid out below and to the north.

Above: Hayburn Wyke from Hayburn Beck.

Right: Hayburn Wyke from Little Cliff.

SUGGESTED SHORT WALKS

Hayburn Wyke and Cloughton Wyke   (4 ½ miles / 7.2 km)

This walk offers a chance to explore the quieter stretch of coastline between Ravenscar and Scarborough. There are great views back to Scarborough Castle and an opportunity to visit the secluded cove at Hayburn Wyke.

The walk begins in Cloughton village and follows Newlands Lane and Salt Pans Road past Court Green Farm and over the old railway line to Cloughton Wyke. While you can follow the lane to its demise at the coast, a more appealing approach to Cloughton Wyke is to take the footpath on the right which strikes out across a field and then turns left along the shallow valley to arrive at Cloughton Wyke. Cloughton Wyke is a little gem of a cove and you will probably have it to yourself, the crowds will be in Scarborough or Robin Hood's Bay.

The route now takes The Cleveland Way along the coastal clifftop path north to Hayburn Wyke. There are lots of ups and downs on this section, but the effort is well repaid with excellent views back to Scarborough Castle and Filey Brigg. On a clear day you will be able to make out Flamborough Head on the other side of Filey Bay.

The path continues above wooded Little Cliff giving a glimpse down into Hayburn Wyke, a sheltered, rocky cove. The path is waymarked down to the rocky shore where Hayburn Beck tumbles over gritstone boulders into the North Sea.

Left: Ancient oak woodland, Hayburn Wyke National Trust woodlands.

Below: Hundale Scar from Cloughton Wyke with the rock pavements below the cliff.

Hayburn Beck waterfall, Hayburn Wyke.

A path climbs up from Hayburn Wyke to the welcome sight of the Hayburn-wyke Hotel. After the climb from the cove you may well be in need of some refreshment. The route back to Cloughton is very straightforward, which might be helpful if you've indulged in some refreshment! Take the old railway line from the site of Hayburn Wyke Station. The platform is just about still visible amongst the vegetation and the stationmaster's house is now a private residence. Opened on 16 July 1885, the railway line between Scarborough and Whitby fell victim to the Beeching Axe and both the station and the route closed on 8 March 1965. The cinder trackbed heads south through farmland back to the bridge we used earlier on Salt Pans Road.

Rock pavement, Salt Pans, Cloughton Wyke.

Cloughton Wyke   (4 ½ miles / 7 km)

Scarborough Castle from Crook Ness.

This is an energetic walk that offers grand views back down the coast to Scarborough Castle and to enjoy the quiet cove of Cloughton Wyke.

The walk starts at the car park at Cloughton Wyke and immediately joins The Cleveland Way to follow the coastal path around the southern edge of Cloughton Wyke. The clifftop path continues on to Hundale Point and then heads south towards the coastguard lookout point at Long Nab.

After the steep drop into Crook Ness, the walk leaves The Cleveland Way to the join the lane from Crook Ness car park to Cliff Top Farm. Head left on Field Lane to the old railway bridge and then climb up to the trackbed to head north on the old Scarborough to Whitby railway line.

The walk soon approaches the old Cloughton Station which is now a tearoom. An old railway coach is preserved on the site. Crossing a road, the walk re-joins the old railway line and continues on to a road overbridge near Cloughton. We take our leave of the railway line here and climb up to the road, turning left to cross the bridge and follow the lane back to the car park at Cloughton Wyke.

Little Cliff, a classic undercliff, seen from Rodger Trod.

Burniston Wyke looking to Scarborough Castle.

Cromer Point and Long Nab from Scalby Ness.

CHAPTER 7
RAVENSCAR TO ROBIN HOOD'S BAY

Grey Seals, Peak Steel, below Ravenscar.

Robin Hood's Bay from Stoupe Brow.

Ravenscar and the Raven Hall Hotel from Stoupe Brow.

Ravenscar is a Victorian enigma. It was originally envisaged to be a seaside resort to rival Scarborough. The arrival of the railway from Whitby to Scarborough in July 1885 had made the concept possible and detailed plans were drafted for houses and hotels. In 1895, the developer John Septimus Bland issued a prospectus and led a group of prominent Yorkshire businessmen in promoting the development of a resort to rival Scarborough. Work started, drains were laid, streets were paved, but the scheme fell through. Location is everything and as attractive a headland as Ravenscar is, the proposed site on the top of a windswept cliff, with difficult access down to a rocky shore, was unlikely to hold popular appeal. It is still possible to see the grid outline of some of the streets planned by the developers. There are just one or two large townhouses that were built that look really incongruous in the open setting.

Today Ravenscar is a quiet place, the railway closed in 1965 and most visitors come for the glorious view over Robin Hood's Bay. The National Trust has a visitor centre here and the adjacent Raven Hall Hotel is popular. In 1774 the Raven Hall Hotel was built as a private residence for Captain William Childs. By 1788 it had been acquired by Doctor Francis Willis. One of its most notable visitors was George III who came here for treatments for his supposed madness. It has been a hotel since 1895. W. H. Hammond, the owner of the Raven Hall Hotel, was not too keen on the railway being visible from his property and insisted on a tunnel rather than the cheaper option of a cutting. The surveyors must have got their calculations wrong because the first attempt at building the tunnel in 1876 emerged on the wrong alignment and it wasn't until 1883 that a replacement tunnel, this time on the correct alignment, was completed.

South Cheek and the Raven Hall Hotel from Stoupe Beck Sands.

Ravenscar and South Cheek from The Nab above the Boggle Hole.

Ravenscar is a geologically fascinating landscape; rocks laid down 160 million years ago in the Jurassic era have influenced the shape of the land as we see it today. Fault lines and geological movement have also played their part in shaping the land, followed by man's influence in the alum quarries that were once abundant here. The Peak Fault, a significant geological fault, raised the land by 600 feet to expose rock strata that would ordinarily be deep underground.

The Peak Fault marks a change in the shape of the coastline. South of Ravenscar the coastline to Scalby Ness is straighter with fewer coves. The cliffs here are formed of the harder Deltaic series of rocks. North of Ravenscar, the coastline reveals a number of scallop-shaped bays as Lias rocks take over. The softer rocks have been lost to sea, while the harder rocks that form the protective headlands – the Nesses – have remained to create the semi-circular bays.

Robin Hood's Bay, Bay Town and North Cheek from Peter White Cliff.

Alum was an important mineral for use in the textile industry. When mixed with urine, the alum would help to 'fix' the dye in cloth and textiles so that it did not run when washed or wet. Boat loads of barrels filled with urine from the London population would make their way up the eastern coast of England. This unpleasant alchemy would then take place at the Low Peak works down below Ravenscar and the processed alum would then be shipped back to the capital for use in the textile mills. Quarried alum was layered with brushwood in large piles. The burnt alum was then steeped in large reservoirs with an alkali to help the liquid crystalize. Other than seaweed, the most readily available alkali was human urine.

It was a process that dates back to Henry VIII's time with quarrying at Ravenscar starting in 1640. As alternative processes were discovered, alum production at Ravenscar finally came to an end in 1862.

The alum reserves lay under shale which is much in evidence along the Yorkshire Coast from Ravenscar to Staithes. Although the quarries were primarily targeting the underlying alum, the shale did not go to waste and would be used for making bricks. Traces of the brick kilns can still be found close to the alum quarries. Whitakers' Brickworks at Ravenscar operated from 1900 to 1939.

Ravenscar is also the final destination of the infamous Lyke Wake Walk, a 40 mile hike across the North York Moors from Osmotherley and intended to be completed within twenty-four hours. The route was devised in 1955 by local farmer Bill Cowley

Low Peak Alum Works.

There are three options to get from Ravenscar to Robin Hood's Bay. The traditional way would be to follow the coastal path, sticking religiously to The Cleveland Way as it clings to the top of the cliffs all the way from below the Raven Hall Hotel. The other option is to follow the old railway line – now known as The Cinder Path – as it winds below Stoupe Brow and on by Fylingthorpe to the old railway station at Robin Hood's Bay. The third, more adventurous option is to climb high above the coast, for perhaps the most spectacular view of Robin Hood's Bay. All three are described in turn here, but before you take your leave of Ravenscar, take some time to seek out a wildlife spectacle.

The Cinder Path, the old railway line, approaching Ravenscar.

Grey Seal hauled out on Peak Steel below Ravenscar.

Grey Seal, Peak Steel.

There is a footpath that leads from below the Raven Hall Hotel, down across the turf of the golf club and into the long grass above the cliffs. Seemingly leading nowhere, stick with the path as it drops down onto the clifftop and then swings right and steeply downhill towards the shore. Care is required, particularly as you approach the rocky shore. The path leads down to the shore between Old Peak (also known as South Cheek) and Peak Steel. If you haven't seen the objective yet, you might have heard a mournful groan rising from the flat rocks around Peak Steel and Low Nook. At various times of day, low tide is the best time, a large group of grey seals can be found hauled out on the rocks, drying themselves and dozing between meals. The colony is a relatively recent addition and in November and December some of the grey seals will come on to shore here to pup. The seals are shy creatures and best observed from a respectful distance. Bulls, females and pups can all be found here from time to time.

Climbing steeply and carefully back up the way we came, the path swings around the perimeter of the golf course and then drops down towards Low Peak Alum Works. Low Peak is now in the care of the National Trust, as is so much of the Yorkshire coastline. What remains today are the ruins of the old works where alum was prepared. It offers a grand place to look out across Robin Hood's Bay. Arrive here on a warm spring or hot summer's morning and you might be lucky enough to find a basking adder. These are shy creatures, but they will start their day sunning themselves to warm the blood enough to head out hunting for small mammals and birds in the undergrowth. They are very shy and will most likely slink away if they hear you coming. Slow worms can be found here too and occasionally both reptiles will bask side by side. Seeing two of our six native reptiles is a real treat on the coastal walk.

The path continues beyond the old Alum Works and along the clifftops above Miller's Nab and High Scar to Peter White Cliff. Beyond here the path joins the steep lane that runs down to Stoupe Bank Farm and drops rapidly to Stoupe Beck. Climbing back up again the path runs on to The Boggle Hole where Mill Beck runs into the sea. Boggle is most probably derived from a local name for a hobgoblin or elfin-type creature. Corruptions of the name occur across northern Britain, from the Boggart of Pots and Pans in Saddleworth to Boggart Hill near Leeds. It also has associations with our more familiar bogeyman. The Boggle Hole was also once the haunt of smugglers. Perhaps the hobgoblin was an invention to keep curious folk away from this area so that the smugglers could move their contraband without fear of disturbance.

Right: Female adder, Low Peak Alum Works.
Far right: Slow Worm, Low Peak Alum Works.
Below: Bay Town from the Boggle Hole.

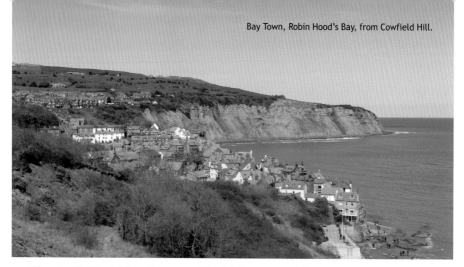

The Youth Hostel is a former mill which operated for 250 years, grinding flour powered by Mill Beck until closure led to a change of use.

Here, if the tide is out, it's possible to drop down onto the beach and finish the final stretch into Robin Hood's Bay along the sands. This is also a popular place with families, the rock pools around High Scar and Stoupe Beck Sands being particularly popular. If the tide is in the footpath continues along the clifftops by Cowfield Hill to emerge in the back lanes of Robin Hood's Bay.

An alternative to the cliff top path is to join the old railway line at Ravenscar and follow this all the way to Robin Hood's Bay. Closed in March 1965, we are indeed fortunate today that we can still enjoy the views once experienced by rail travellers of old, as the path is now a popular walking and cycle way, known as The Cinder Path. The railway was single track and there is still evidence to be found, the old over bridges and occasionally some sleepers still remain.

Bay Town and North Cheek, Robin Hood's Bay from The Nab above the Boggle Hole.

The Cinder Path is a great alternative to the coastal path with easier gradients, the Victorian surveyors selecting a winding route to ensure heavy trains could climb the banks. In spring and early summer the path is lined with gorse bushes giving off a heady, buttery scent, reminiscent of butterscotch. Look closely and you might find some gorse shield bugs, though they are expertly camouflaged. There is a small nature reserve in the old alum quarry here and from time to time roe deer can be spotted amongst the trees and shrubs.

The Cinder Path winds above Stoupe Brow Farm, but below Stoupe Brow itself, swinging west from Susannah Hill to cross under a road and then head further west past Browside Farm to Howdale Wood. Heading across Stoupe Beck in Allison Head Wood, the route now swings north and then towards the north and east to pass Fyling Old Hall and then to cross Ramsdale Beck on its journey into Robin Hood's Bay along the edge of Fylingthorpe.

An energetic alternative to the coastal path and Cinder Path is to climb high onto Stoupe Brow. This is a superb vantage point and for those undertaking the coastal walk in late August or the first week of September, it is highly recommended, particularly for those with an interest in our past.

A path leaves the old railway line just beyond Ravenscar to climb steeply past Church Farm to a lane. Heading right the lane expires at another farm and group of cottages where a path climbs steeply on the edge of Open Access land to Beacon Howes on Scarborough Road.

Right: Sandwich terns, Stoupe Beck Sands.

Below: Robin Hood's Bay from the Cinder Path on Susannah Hill. Low tide reveals the concentric rings of the scars on the seashore.

This is a superb section and when the heather is in bloom, a deep purple haze provides a foreground to a stunning vista of the wide sweep of Robin Hood's Bay. This is a glorious spot to linger and enjoy perhaps the best view of Robin Hood's Bay, enhanced by the flowering ling. Bell heather might well be still in bloom here too, as it tends to flower in late July and early August. Green Dike, an ancient earthwork, is still clearly visible on the ground.

From the car park near the trig point, a permissive path heads out across the heather on Open Access land, shown on maps as a dotted black line. A leaflet is available online that describes where to find some of the Bronze Age features. A huge moorland fire on this stretch of Fylingdales Moor in 2003 revealed some of these features of the past and it's still possible to see them now before the heather grows back. There are flat rocks with Bronze Age rock art, distinctive cup and ring markings carved into the gritstone, there are standing stones and burial tumuli. The most distinctive tumuli are the groups of three known as Robin Hood's Butts.

Also to be found are distinctive sledways, hollowed ways carved out over the decades as pony-hauled sleds were used to haul quarried stone off the moor.

The permissive path heads out across the moor on a track towards Stoupe Brow and Home Farm. The route drops steeply down on one of the old holloways

where the sleds have eroded huge deep ruts into the stone, a rare example of an ancient rutway in this part of the country. From here you can rejoin The Cinder Path railway trackbed or there are a number of field paths that take you back to the coastal path.

Left: Bronze Age rock art and a burial mound or tumulus, Stoupe Brow.

Below: Robin Hood's Bay from Stoupe Brow.

SUGGESTED SHORT WALKS

Stoupe Brow   (2 miles / 3.2 km)

This walk is a brief circuit of the Bronze Age and Neolithic archaeological treasures that were revealed by a devastating moorland fire in the summer of 2003. The heather has since recovered and August makes a particularly attractive time of year for the walk.

The walk starts at the parking area near the telecoms mast on Beacon Howes, just off Scarborough Road above Ravenscar. It's worth crossing the road briefly to appraise the view of Robin Hood's Bay from Green Dike. This is a superb panorama and must rank as one of the best views on the Yorkshire Coast. It is enhanced even further in August or early September when the ling heather is in bloom and a purple haze provides a stunning foreground to the sweep of Robin Hood's Bay.

Above: Bronze Age rock art. Cup marks carved into an earthfast boulder, Stoupe Brow.

Below: Sled way, Stoupe Brow. Grooves have been carved into this great slab of rock to ease the passage of sledges laden with stone from the quarries on Stoupe Brow.

Return to the parking area which was once the site of a Second World War radar station, where a path leads off in a north-westerly direction through the heather. After about 300 yards the path crosses a track and continues in the same direction across Stoupe Brow.

The track passes a low burial mound, shown as a tumulus on the Ordnance Survey map, one of a number revealed by the fire. It is thought to be about 3900 years old. As with many of these Bronze Age burial cairns, this one has been excavated by antiquarians in the recent past.

The route passes a number of hollow ways where pony-drawn sledges have worn a depression while carrying materials and supplies to and from the alum quarries below Stoupe Brow.

The track continues on past Robin Hood's Butts, a group of three early Bronze Age burial mounds. It was typical for Bronze Age tribes to bury their dead in these tumuli on high ground and they certainly chose well, as the view across Robin Hood's Bay to North Cheek is stunning.

Located nearby is a flat stone with traces of Neolithic rock art. Thought to be almost 5000 years old, two cup marks can be traced on the stone. A cairn on the brow offers further grand views down to Bay Town and Robin Hood's Bay before the track sweeps to the left. A short standing stone helps to locate another Bronze Age ring cairn.

Look out for a thin path heading left off the main track. This passes another Bronze Age cairn with a low standing stone and then crosses a shallow ditch. Where the path bends left another flat stone has a number of cups and grooves carved in the surface. These are about 5000 years old. The path heads for a burial mound and passes another earthfast boulder with cups and grooves carved in it. Passing the large burial mound, the footpath meets up with the outward route and turns right back to the start.

Robin Hood's Bay from Stoupe Brow.

North Cheek across Robin Hood's Bay from South Cheek.

Ravenscar   (5 miles / 8km)

This is a short walk that takes in sweeping views of Robin Hood's Bay, enjoys a brief visit to the Low Peak Alum Works and follows the old Scarborough to Whitby railway line.

Starting from Ravenscar, follow the path downhill from the National Trust visitor centre to join the old railway line which ran from Scarborough to Whitby. The Cinder Path is now a popular cycle and walking route and offers great views of the coast. It would undoubtedly be a popular railway today for day trippers if it had survived the Beeching Axe. The last train ran on 8 March 1965, but at least today we can still enjoy views from this old route and so the efforts of those Victorian navvies were not in vain.

We follow the trackbed for a good 2 miles with tempting views of Robin Hood's Bay. For much of spring the bright yellow gorse bushes will be in flower, giving off a sweet buttery scent.

At Browhill Farm the walk leaves The Cinder Path and heads downhill across a field to cross a footbridge over a stream and then head into thin woodland. Turning right onto Bridge Holm Lane the route heads downhill to meet the coast at Boggle Hole.

From here our route follows The Cleveland Way coastal path along the clifftops south to Stoupe Brow Cottage and then continues again on the Cleveland Way to Low Peak Alum Works. Now in the care of the National Trust, it's worth taking some time to explore these old ruins and maybe spot an adder or slow worm basking.

South Cheek, Ravenscar from Peter White Cliff.

From here the route climbs back up the steep hill into Ravenscar.

Robin Hood's Bay from Ravenscar with the famous concentric rings of the sea bed revealed at low tide.
Bay Town from the beach at Boggle Hole.

CHAPTER 8

ROBIN HOOD'S BAY TO WHITBY

Saltwick Nab at sunset on the summer solstice from Saltwick Sands.

Whitby's 1858 built-lighthouse below Ling Hill.

Robin Hood's Bay is the jewel in the Yorkshire Coast and therefore attracts scores of visitors on a sunny summer Sunday. Along with those arriving by car and bus, many will have walked in on the coastal path from Whitby or from Ravenscar, but there may well be a few who are dipping their boots in the North Sea down on the sands. These ramblers might well have come all the way from St Bees on the Cumbrian Coast as Robin Hood's Way is at the end of the famous Coast to Coast Walk devised in 1969 and published in 1973 by Alfred Wainwright. It's a fitting end to such a huge expedition, a real incentive to those trekking across the high North York Moors in the closing miles of their 192-mile pilgrimage.

Notwithstanding whether a character such as Robin Hood ever existed at all or whether the folk legend is a composite of characters from history, it is unlikely that Robin Hood ever came to this part of North Yorkshire. There is an old folk ballad that tells the tale of Robin Hood taking on a group of French pirates who had looted the North East Coast and stolen the fishing boats from the local fishermen. The pirates surrendered to Robin Hood who, true to form, returned the pirate's loot back to the poor people in the village that we know of today as Robin Hood's Bay. Another similar tale proposes that Robin Hood helped the Abbott of Whitby to repel Scandinavian raiders and a further version suggests that the villagers helped to hide Robin Hood away while he was on the run from King John's troops. The name was recorded as early as 1536 when the village was recorded as having 50 fishing boats. By 1886, the fleet had grown to 174 as the herring industry along the Yorkshire Coast exploded.

Left: Bay Town and The Bay Hotel - the end of the Coast to Coast Walk.

Below: King Street, Bay Town.

Sunny Place, Bay Town, one of many delightful snickelways.

An old wartime mine, from the top of Bay Town looking towards Stoupe Brow.

Robin Hood's Bay is a real jumble of picture postcard cottages with red pantiled roofs. There are hidden alleyways, snickets and ginnels which are a pleasure to explore. When bathed in sunshine it's easy to imagine you're on holiday down on the Cornish Riviera. There are few cars down in Bay Town, as the village is properly known, with everyone encouraged to park at the old railway station at the top of the town. A sad fate for a railway that would have undoubtedly been a spectacular way to enjoy the coast today. The railway closed in 1965.

Robin Hood's Bay had a reputation for being at the heart of the smuggling trade on the Yorkshire Coast and its network of alleyways and maze of tiny streets would undoubtedly help smugglers evaporate in the night when pursued by customs officials. Smuggling peaked in the late eighteenth century. In 1779 a pitched battle between customs and excise offices and smugglers took place in the village, fighting over 200 casks of brandy and gin and fifteen sacks of tea. Six years earlier, as an illustration of how organised smuggling was, the two customs cutters the *Mermaid* and the *Eagle* were outgunned and routed from Robin Hood's Bay by three smugglers' vessels. Legend has it that contraband could be smuggled from the beach to the top of the town without ever seeing the light of day.

Ravenscar and Robin Hood's Bay seen from Bay Town.   Ravenscar and Robin Hood's Bay from above Bay Town.

There's a lifeboat museum down by the quayside and plenty of places to grab something to eat, from the fish and chip shop to the various pubs that line the steep streets that lead down to the front.

Robin Hood's Bay has seen its fair share of shipwrecks. This stretch of coastline can be treacherous for shipping. In 1881 the *Visitor*, a collier working between Tyneside and London, was caught in a storm off Flamborough Head. The strong winds and currents drove the stricken vessel north to Robin Hood's Bay. On 19 January, the *Visitor* was abandoned by its crew as it had started to take on a significant amount of water. Soon after, the *Visitor* sank. The crew had managed to get into their lifeboat, but were still in peril on the high sea.

The Whitby lifeboat couldn't launch from Whitby because of heavy seas and it was just not possible to row the lifeboat out of Whitby harbour. The remarkable decision was taken to launch the lifeboat from Robin Hood's Bay. The lifeboat was dragged 8 miles across country from Whitby to Robin Hood's Bay. Hauled in its cradle by a team of eleven horses and sixty men, it being January, the roads were under deep snow with drifts 7 feet high in places.

Robin Hood's Bay from St Stephen's churchyard.

Starfish, Robin Hood's Bay.

By early afternoon the team had managed to descend the narrow streets of Robin Hood's Bay with the lifeboat and were ready to launch. The storm was still raging and the first wave broke six of the massive oars and injured two lifeboat-men. New oars were found and the eighteen-strong lifeboat crew headed out into the raging waters once more. This time they succeeded and managed to bring the six crew from the *Visitor* safely ashore.

When the tide is out, Robin Hood's Bay is a popular spot for rock pooling. Here you will find the four main species of crab that are common on the East Coast: hermit crabs, brown crabs (sometimes known as edible crabs), green or shore crabs and if you are particularly lucky, the lovely blue-coloured velvet swimming crab. If you don't find the actual crab, you will inevitably find an empty carapace or severed pincers, a sure sign that the crab met an unfortunate end, possibly at the hands of a grey seal or the beak of a herring gull. Other than crabs you are most likely to find periwinkles, anenomes and shrimps.

The bay is geologically interesting and when viewed from the cliffs above Ravenscar, when the tide is out, the bay is a series of concentric rock rings, carved out over time by thousands and thousands of advancing and retreating tides.

Brown or edible Crab, Robin Hood's Bay.   Sea anemone, Robin Hood's Bay.

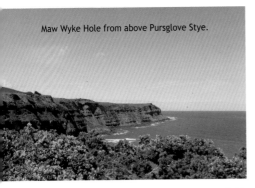

Maw Wyke Hole from above Pursglove Stye.

It's a very steep climb back out of Bay Town up to the top of the town. The old railway line – now known as The Cinder Path – leads directly back to Whitby inland from the coast and makes for a useful circular route. The coastal path heads out in parallel with the trackbed of the railway line and re-joins the cliff. There is an old rocket post here that was used for practising the rocket launching of lifebelts or breeches buoys to stricken vessels.

The path continues along the cliffs to North Cheek or Ness Point, the northern arm of the protective semi-circle of cliffs that shelters Robin Hood's Bay from the worst of the weather. Notwithstanding the natural protection of the cliffs, Robin Hood's Bay has suffered at the hands of savage coastal storms in the past and in 1975 a concrete sea wall was built to protect the cottages and houses. The most disastrous storm was in 1780 when a huge cliff-fall took many houses from King Street with it.

From here on, the cliff-top path passes scores of intriguingly named features marked on the map, but not so obvious on the ground. Bulmer Steel, Castle Chamber, Cow & Calf, Craze Naze, Clock Case Nab, Far Jetticks, Normanby Stye Batts and White Horse. What imagination the folk who used to live here had when conveying the names of these local features to the first Ordnance Survey men who came this way to map the coast.

Normanby Stye from Clock Case Nab.

Whitby lighthouse, Ling Hill.

The coastal path continues across Oakham Beck below Hawsker Bottoms and on to Gnipe Howe and Widdy Head. At Whitestone Point below Ling Hill we encounter Whitby lighthouse. This tall white structure was built in 1858. Like so many lighthouses, it was automated in 1992. Still owned by Trinity House, it is now possible to stay here, the ancillary buildings converted into holiday cottages.

It's also possible to stay in the adjacent fog signal station, also known as the Hawsker Bull. This operated from 1902 to 1988. Two huge black horns on the flat roof of the station bellowed out a deep throaty warning when a sea fret moved in. A sea fret, sometimes called a haar, is a cold sea fog common to the east coast of England and Scotland. It occurs when warmer moist air moves over the cooler North Sea. This causes the moisture in the air to condense, forming the sea fret.

The sea fret then rolls in over the clifftops and heads inland. The temperature drops markedly and visibility is reduced to a matter of yards. A sea fret typically occurs between April and September. It can be hot and sunny further inland, but cold and foggy on the coast. It can be quite an eerie experience watching a fret slowly advance towards the coast from off the sea and envelop coastal communities.

Pursglove Stye Batts from Widdy Head.

Saltwick Bay from Saltwick Cliffs.

Wreck of the trawler *Admiral Von Tromp*,
Saltwick Bay.

Wreck of the MV *Creteblock*, The Scar, Whitby.

Just a little further on along the coastal cliffs another highlight of this section is revealed in Saltwick Bay. Saltwick Bay is protected by two large rock outcrops, both comprised of shale. Black Nab looks for all the world like a surfacing submarine with the nab itself reminiscent of the conning tower. When seen from Black Nab, Saltwick Nab looks uncannily like a sperm whale. It is fascinating that two natural geological features should take on the form of a whale and a submarine. Wholly appropriate somehow.

Saltwick Bay is a particularly popular place with photographers and it is well worth a detour down the steps to the beach. Visit in June or early July when sunset coincides with low tide and you are likely to find a gaggle of photographers with tripods scuttling about the flat rocks and tidal pools. In high summer, although we are on the east coast, it's possible to watch the sun both rise and set over the North Sea at this point as the coast has turned east to west rather than north to south. It's a spectacular sight as the sun slowly sinks behind Saltwick Nab, emphasising the sperm whale outline.

The wreck of an old fishing vessel, the *Admiral Von Tromp*, adds foreground interest to those photographs. The boat was wrecked at Saltwick in October 1976. This is another great place for fossil hunting, ammonites and belemnites being particularly common in the shale.

Beyond Saltwick Bay the coastal path passes through a static caravan site, one of a small number on the coastal route with an enviable location. Passing by Saltwick Bay, the route climbs above The Scar. If the tide is out or the water not too deep you will see the broken wreck of the MV *Creteblock*.

Whitby Abbey and the North York Moors from above The Scar.

When steel was in short supply during the First World War, a novel idea was to build ships from reinforced concrete and rather remarkably the idea worked. MV *Creteblock* was built at Shoreham in Kent in 1919, too late to see active service, but it saw use as a tug boat until 1934 when it was brought to Whitby for dismantling. This didn't take place and the MV *Creteblock* deteriorated in condition until 1947 when the decision was made to tow her out into deep water and scuttle her. The boat sank in the shallow water where she rests today and explosives were later used to break her up. When viewed from the clifftop path, the MV *Creteblock* still displays the clear outline of a boat.

One of the greatest tragedies off the coast of Whitby was the loss of the hospital ship *Rohilla* in 1914. Built in 1905 as a passenger steamer, *Rohilla* worked for the British India Steam Navigation Company. She was enlisted into military service at the start of the First World War as a hospital ship, although had also spent time as a troopship prior to the outbreak of war. Unfortunately she ran aground in October 1914 at Saltwick Nab with the loss of 83 lives.

By now the skeletal remains of St Hilda's Abbey at Whitby are in view, backed by rolling heather moorland. There are grand views inland down the length of the Esk Valley. There can be countless days when moody clouds hang over the North York Moors, yet the coast is bathed in sunshine beneath clear blue skies.

The path crosses a green and past the old Whitby Cross to arrive in St Mary's churchyard and an exhilarating arrival into Whitby, laid out below.

Whitby Abbey from above The Scar.

SUGGESTED SHORT WALKS

Robin Hood's Bay   (4 ¾ miles / 7.6 km)

This walk explores the delights of Bay Town, the maze of streets and alleyways that thread the jumble of cottages that make up this attractive village. It then climbs up to head along the coast with excellent views across Robin Hood's Bay to Ravenscar. The return leg is along The Cinder Path, the old railway line from Whitby to Scarborough.

Parking up in the old station car park, there is an option to visit Bay Town either at the beginning or end of the walk. Either way you have to make the steep descent and ascent.

The walk joins The Cleveland Way opposite the car park in Mount Pleasant North and immediately heads into the field where there is a replica rocket post. These were used for practising the launch of breeches buoys to assist a rescue from stricken vessels. The Cleveland Way heads out along the cliff-top path with superb views south across Robin Hood's Bay to Ravenscar. This is a good spot from which to appraise this geologically fascinating bowl.

The path then sweeps around the cliff tops to the north crossing Rain Dale before continuing above the cliffs to Limekiln Slack. We leave the coastal cliff top path here and take the permissive path that strikes out west across a field to join the old railway line. Turn left on the old railway line to head south on a good quality path that leads unfailingly back into Robin Hood's Bay, again offering excellent views across the bay.

Right: Robin Hood's Bay from The Cinder Path on North Cheek.

Below: Widdy Head from Gnipe Howe.

Whitby and Saltwick Bay   (5 miles / 8 km)

This is a walk that offers a grand approach to Whitby from the south, a dramatically sighted lighthouse and a chance to visit St Hilda's Abbey. Starting from the railway station, bus station or large car park by the harbour, the walk heads across the swingbridge and follows Church Road. Look out for steps on the left to climb Boulby Bank to turn left onto a road – The Ropery. The route heads straight across Green Lane to follow steps and a path to join New Gardens Lane. Continue on past Flatts Farm on the lane to Hawsker Lane.

Black Nab from Saltwick Bay.

Turn right along Hawsker Lane for about ½ mile and then turn left on a track that leads past Brook House and Ling Hill Farm. From here the lane swings right below Ling Hill to a grand arrival at Whitby lighthouse at Whitestone Point. A stone stile gives access to the coastal path and route finding from here to Whitby is very straightforward.

The path continues along the clifftops to Saltwick Bay, offering sweeping views out to sea and some beautiful coastal scenery. At Saltwick Bay, a sloping path and then steps from the right hand side of the caravan park entrance offer a chance for a more intimate exploration of Saltwick Bay. If the tide is out this is a good place for fossil hunting and to examine the two Nabs that bookend the bay – Black Nab and Saltwick Nab.

Otherwise, continue through the caravan park – the route is clearly waymarked – to rejoin the clifftop path above Saltwick Nab. Look out for the wreck of MV *Creteblock* down on the rocks below around The Scar.

Saltwick Bay from Saltwick Cliffs.

The skeletal remains of St Hilda's Abbey are now clearly in sight and to the west the rolling North York Moors and the Esk Valley that flows into the sea at Whitby. There are grand views across Whitby's two piers to Sandsend Ness.

The cliff-top path leads unfailingly on to the green in front of Whitby Abbey. Whitby Cross stands tall on the green. This is a good opportunity to visit Whitby Abbey; the entrance is on the left. Otherwise the route continues past St Mary's churchyard down the 199 Steps to enter Whitby old town on Church Street. Either Church Street or Sandgate will take you back to the swingbridge over the River Esk.

Left: An RAF Sea King helicopter on exercise, Black Nab, Saltwick Bay.

Below: Sandwich Terns, Saltwick Bay.

Saltwick Nab from Saltwick Bay.

Saltwick Nab from Saltwick Sands.

CHAPTER 9
WHITBY

Upper harbour, Whitby from West Quay.

East Cliff, Whitby from West Pier.

Whitby Abbey.

Swingbridge over the River Esk from West Cliff, Whitby.

Wonderful Whitby. Whitby is a real gem of a place, Norse in origin – the suffix '-by' being a big clue and clearly an obvious place for Viking sailors to make land when arriving in Yorkshire, then part of Northumbria.

There are two distinct halves to Whitby, bisected by the tidal River Esk. The eastern half, with the Old Town, the Abbey and St Mary's church has real olde world charm; the western half is classic Victorian seaside resort, particularly up on West Cliff. Below there is an array of fish and chip shops, amusement arcades, cockle and mussel stalls and kiss-me-quick style souvenir shops on the quayside.

Whitby is busy at any time of year, but particularly so on a summer weekend. There's no end of season these days though and a sunny day in autumn or winter can still draw the crowds, along with the Goth Weekend around Halloween when you are likely to encounter some unusual darkly-dressed characters roaming the town.

A good place to start in Whitby is the swingbridge in the centre of town. There has been a bridge on this site since at least 1351 when reference was made to a toll bridge. In 1629 a proposal was made to replace the existing wooden bridge with one that had moving parts. It is known that in later years there was a drawbridge which in turn was replaced with a swingbridge in 1833. The current bridge was built in 1908. Recently refurbished, the bridge is vital to the functioning of Whitby and it causes a real headache when it fails. It opens regularly throughout the day to allow boats with masts through.

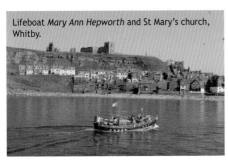
Lifeboat *Mary Ann Hepworth* and St Mary's church, Whitby.

Fishing boat, Whitby harbour.

The Old Town is a real gem, full of independent shops and you certainly won't be short of anywhere to buy a piece of jet jewellery. Jet is synonymous with Whitby and there have been jet workshops and jet shops in Whitby for a long time, though it became infinitely more popular and fashionable when Queen Victoria chose to wear it as part of her trademark black costume. At its height, up to 1500 people were working in the Whitby jet industry. It was the Romans who first discovered the ornamental possibilities of jet.

Grape Lane, Old Town, Whitby.

Start by exploring Grape Lane, home to the Captain Cook Museum and then it's worth an exploration of Sandgate, Church Street, Tate Hill and Henrietta Street around the Old Town. The original Town Hall with its distinctive clock tower overlooks the small market square. The Town Hall was built in 1788 for Nathaniel Cholmley. The Cholmley family were large landowners in the area having purchased much of Whitby from King Henry VIII after the Dissolution of the Monasteries. Their family hall is now part of the English Heritage site next to the Abbey.

Henrietta Street which reaches out to the East Pier takes its name from Nathaniel Cholmley's wife. Up until 1761 it was known as Haggerlythe, a much more Scandinavian name. This area of Whitby has seen continual cliff falls with many houses lost to landslips over the last 200 years and heavy rains in recent years have led to further spectacular falls. During a great storm in 2014, part of the graveyard of St Mary's church above was exposed and skeletons from the graves were deposited down in the gardens of the houses below.

Captain Cook Museum, Grape Lane, Whitby Old Town.

1788-built Town Hall, Old Town, Whitby.

Church Street, Old Town, Whitby.

Above left: Arguments Yard, Old Town, Whitby.

Above right: Jet Shop, Church Street, Old Town, Whitby.

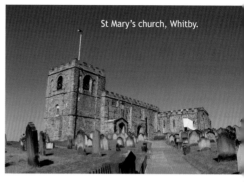

St Mary's church, Whitby.

199 steps, also known as Church Stairs, Whitby.

There are innumerable yards and alleyways in the Old Town, the best of which is the intriguingly named Arguments Yard. Not a place to linger if you're feeling a bit stressed.

There are a few options here, climbing the 199 steps (or the adjacent Donkey Road) to St Mary's church and Whitby Abbey or heading out past the old smokehouse to the eastern pier. It will be hard to resist the temptation to count the number of steps, just in case someone got their sums wrong. Don't lose count; otherwise it's a heart busting double return trip to count them all over again. Work started on these stone steps in 1702 replacing an earlier wooden staircase. At the top of the 199 steps you reach Caedmon's Cross, commemorating the father of the modern hymn. Caedmon was a Saxon herdsman and would compose poems and songs in praise of his god. He later became a monk at the adjacent Abbey. The cross itself was erected in 1898.

St Mary's church is a real gem, dating from the twelfth century, it has an attractive honey coloured stone exterior, but a trip inside will be a real surprise. Built in 1110, it replaced an earlier Saxon wooden chapel and incorporates some classic Norman features. The tower was added in 1170 and in 1225 the north transept was built. A south transept was added in 1380 to complete the current cruciform shape of the church. The interior is fascinating, box pews and wooden stairs, pulpits, panelling and suspended wooden walkways, largely dating to the seventeenth and eighteenth centuries. There is a three-storey pulpit to seek out and an early Victorian hearing aid.

St Mary's church, Whitby.

It's worth a trip around the graveyard too, for this is where Bram Stoker's black dog is supposed to have come up to after landing from the *Demeter* before transforming into Dracula. The graveyard is home to wildlife and common shrews can be regularly found around the tombstones, some of which display the skull and crossbones, not that these are pirate graves; this was once a symbol of mortality.

Just beyond the churchyard is Whitby Abbey and if you're lucky, an old Series II Landrover from the 1960s, converted to an ice cream van, will be doing a roaring trade.

St Hilda's Abbey is in the care of English Heritage. There has been an abbey on this site since AD657 when St Hilda founded the Abbey, though the current remains largely date to the thirteenth century. This is where the General Synod set the date of Easter, way back in AD664, when they decided that Easter should fall on the first Sunday after the first full moon after the vernal equinox and this has governed the fortunes of the British Bank Holiday experience ever since.

The Abbey's dominant position on the cliff tops made it a target for Viking raids and the first abbey was destroyed in AD867. In 1067, a Norman knight, Reinfrid established a new abbey which took almost 300 years to build, but like abbeys and priories across the country, the Dissolution of the Monasteries during the Reformation led to the destruction of the Abbey in 1549. The north transept still presents a striking image even in partial ruin.

Far left:
Whitby Abbey.

Left: Whitby Abbey during the Whitby Illuminated event.

Whitby Abbey during Whitby Illuminated.

St Hilda was originally Princess Hild from Hartlepool and when she arrived in town, Whitby was then known as Streoneshalh. It was the Vikings who would later bestow the name Whitby on this place, -by being a common Norse suffix. The first abbey on the site was a wooden structure known as St Peter's. Long after her death, when Hild had become the patron saint of Whitby, the Abbey would later take her name.

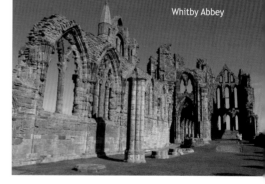
Whitby Abbey

As with Scarborough, Whitby came under heavy bombardment from a German battlecruiser *Derflinger* out in the North Sea in 1914. The Abbey was partly damaged during this attack. It had already suffered badly from being plundered for stone and the central tower had collapsed in 1830.

The Abbey is particularly popular during the Goth Weekend, but it is an atmospheric place to linger at any time of year, particularly in the autumn when a sea fret can transform Whitby on a sunny day into a cold, eerie, quiet place. Occasionally in October and November, the Abbey runs an Illuminated event when the ruins are bathed in a palette of primary colours and dramatic lighting.

Returning back down the 199 steps, it's worth paying a visit to the smokehouse to stock up on genuine Whitby kippers. This is one of the few traditional smokehouses left on the Yorkshire Coast.

Beyond here it is still possible to drop down to the old eastern stone pier which dates to 1702. The walkway to the outer pier collapsed in the 1990s, but this is a good place to come and appraise Whitby away from crowds.

Another good pier to explore on the eastern half is Tate Hill Pier with its giant rusting anchor.

Back over the swingbridge brings you to the promenade. This is the busier half of Whitby and there are some wonderful fish and chip shops on this section where you can either eat in or get a takeaway. The most famous of these is the Magpie Café, clearly a place of pilgrimage for devotees of that most British of takeaway meals. The queue out of the door on most days through spring and summer and almost every weekend is a testament to the quality of what is on offer inside.

Tate Hill Pier below St Mary's church.

East Pier and the 1854-built lighthouse.

East Pier, Whitby.

The Magpie Café, West Quay.

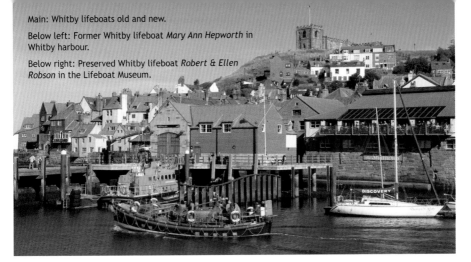

Main: Whitby lifeboats old and new.

Below left: Former Whitby lifeboat *Mary Ann Hepworth* in Whitby harbour.

Below right: Preserved Whitby lifeboat *Robert & Ellen Robson* in the Lifeboat Museum.

With your fish and chips, a good place to head for is the western pier. It's still possible to access the wooden western pier and this is a popular Sunday stroll. The first piers were built in the sixteenth century, but West Pier was rebuilt in stone in 1814. The piers were cleverly designed to prevent the largest waves entering the harbour and they still do a remarkably good job of protecting Whitby from the worst ravages of the North Sea.

The lighthouse on West Pier was built in 1831 and towers 83 feet over the adjacent pier. That on East Pier is much shorter at 54 feet and was built later in 1854.

Whitby is famous for its lifeboats and the lifeboat museum sits at the bottom of West Cliff, where the lifeboat *Robert and Ellen Robson* is on display inside. This rowing lifeboat served from 1947 to 1957. The *Mary Ann Hepworth* which served from 1938 to 1974 is used to operate tourist trips around the harbour and just out into the sea beyond the piers.

Whitby is still home to a sizeable fishing fleet and trawlers and fishing vessels can often be seen moored along the various quaysides around the town along the River Esk. If they are not there, the fishermen will be braving the North Sea to bring in the catch. Boat repairs still take place in Whitby and it's also a popular mooring for leisure craft. The River Esk is tidal and salmon still make their way upstream to spawn, along with the occasional grey seal and otter.

Whitby trades on the heritage experience and on any given weekend you will hear a steam whistle. It will probably be from the railway station that has been recently expanded to allow more steam trains to run to and from the nearby North York Moors Railway. This offers a spectacularly scenic journey through the moors to the market town of Pickering. Regular steam services run from March to October throughout the year. There is also a steam bus around town – *Elizabeth*, an old Sentinel steam waggon dating from 1931. Sometimes you'll see the old Dennis 1929 charabanc *Charlotte* operating trips around the town too.

The railway station still serves the main line rail network and regular trains run to Middlesbrough and Darlington. Whitby also has exceptionally good bus connections which run parallel to the coast, serving the destinations once served by the railways that closed in the 1950s and 1960s. The railway arrived in 1836 and until that point it was a difficult trek across poor moorland roads to reach Whitby. Before the coming of the railway, the easiest way to reach Whitby was by sea. There are regular buses to Scarborough and towards Saltburn and these are particularly handy for walking a linear section of the coastal path.

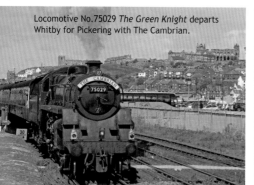

Locomotive No.75029 *The Green Knight* departs Whitby for Pickering with The Cambrian.

Sentinel steam waggon *Elizabeth* on Whitby Pier Road.

1919-Dennis-built charabanc *Charlotte* at Whitby Pier Road.

1958-Bedford-built Duple 'Coast and Country' bus at Whitby harbour.

St Mary's church from the ginnel beneath Whitby West Cliff.

Captain Cook's statue looks out from Whitby West Cliff.

It's worth climbing the steep steps and through the attractive arch tunnel up to West Cliff where a statue of Captain Cook looks out across the harbour from which he served his apprenticeship. We are in Captain Cook country, a loose marketing term for the coast and moors around Whitby, Staithes and inland Great Ayton. James Cook was born in 1728 in Marton near Middlesbrough. He was schooled in Great Ayton before taking an apprenticeship with a draper in the small fishing port of Staithes. It is likely that this is where he developed a keen interest in the sea and the possibilities of adventure. Cook took a job on a coal ship at Whitby in 1747 and eight years later joined the Royal Navy. A scale replica of his ship, the Bark *Endeavour* can be found in the harbour from time to time. It was from Whitby that James Cook made his first voyage. Whitby was once a major shipbuilding centre and Captain James Cook chose Whitby-built ships for his voyages of discovery around the world. All four of his principal ships, the *Endeavour, Resolution, Adventure* and *Discovery* were built in Whitby. Cook met his end at the hands of natives in Hawaii in 1780.

The steep winding road below West Cliff is known as the Khyber Pass and it was cut deep into the rock to ease the gradient for motor vehicles from the quay to the top of the cliff.

Alongside Cook's statue is the whalebone arch, a reminder that Whitby was once at the heart of this brutal trade, when sailing ships would set sail for Arctic waters near Greenland in pursuit of these graceful leviathans of the sea. William Scoresby was perhaps Whitby's most famous whaler. Whaling ceased in 1837 as gas lamps rapidly replaced the need for whale oil and blubber.

The best way to see whales these days is in their natural environment and in the summer months it is still possible to take a whaling trip from Whitby to see and photograph these wonderful marine mammals.

Whitby West Cliff has a distinctly different feel to the Old Town below East Cliff. West Cliff expanded during the railway boom. The railway had arrived in 1836 and George Hudson of the North Eastern Railway realised its potential, promoting the construction of a classic Victorian resort high on the West Cliffs. The regimented, almost American-like, grid plan is a real clue that this part of Whitby was developed from scratch.

Sentinel Steam Wagon *Elizabeth* climbing the Khyber Pass, Whitby West Cliff.

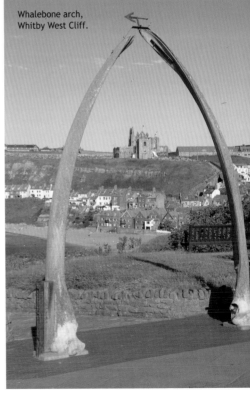

Whalebone arch, Whitby West Cliff.

SUGGESTED SHORT WALK

Whitby Town Trail

Start at the Abbey and pass through St Mary's churchyard to descend the 199 steps of Church Stairs to Henrietta Street. Originally much longer with more than 100 houses, two major landslips in 1787 and 1871 destroyed many properties. The last of Whitby's smokehouses can be found along to the right. Locate the steps down to Tate Hill Pier which offers good views of the harbour and the main East and West Piers.

Trillos of Whitby has been a family-run ice cream business since 1912. Their 1968 Series II Landrover ice cream van is seen at Whitby Abbey.

Tate Hill was the site of Whitby's original East Pier which dated back to the very early seventeenth century. In its time it has also been known as Burgess Pier. The current pier dates from around 1765 and Whitby's lifeboat was kept here from 1822 to 1863.

Return to Church Street where you will find innumerable Whitby jet shops. Jet is fossilized wood from the monkey puzzle tree and can be shaped and polished to produce some very attractive jewellery.

Tate Hill Pier with St Mary's church above.

Continue along Church Street to the White Horse and Griffin public house. This inn was built in the late eighteenth century and is named after the Cholmley family who owned much of Whitby after the Dissolution of the Monasteries. The Cholmleys were influential Lords of the Manor and the griffin was on their coat of arms. The inn was the destination for the first stage coach that operated from York to Whitby and early travellers would have been very relieved to reach the inn after what would inevitably have been a tortuous journey across the high North York Moors. A stiff drink would have been the first request.

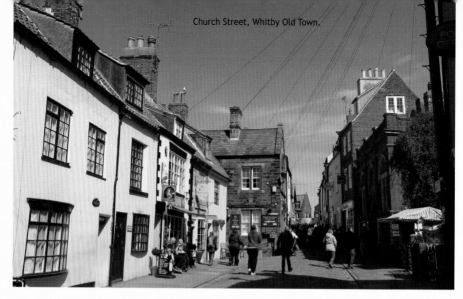

Church Street, Whitby Old Town.

Head along Church Street past the junction and turn right into Grape Lane. The Captain Cook Museum on the left is in a house that in the 1740s belonged to Captain Walker. Walker employed apprentices to learn a trade on sailing ships used to carry coals along the Yorkshire Coast. James Cook was apprenticed to Walker and lived in the attic on his arrival from Staithes in 1746. Cook left nine years later to begin his illustrious career with the Royal Navy.

Cross the swingbridge for a closer look at the harbour and then turn around to retrace steps and turn left into Sandgate.

Turn right to pass the Town Hall, built in 1788 by Jonathan Pickernell. Pickernell had previously worked on the harbour and built the West Pier. The Cholmleys paid for construction of the Town Hall and the adjacent market place which replaced the old market on the opposite side of the river.

Turn left into Church Street to return to the foot of the 199 steps to retrace outward route to the Abbey.

Far left: Captain Cook Museum, Grape Lane, Whitby Old Town.

Left: 199 steps, Church Stairs, Whitby East Cliff.

Locomotive No. 45428 *Eric Treacy* departs Whitby with a train over the North York Moors Railway for Pickering.

Whitby East Cliff, St Mary's church, Old Town and Tate Hill Pier from West Cliff.

CHAPTER 10
WHITBY TO STAITHES

Runswick Bay from Runswick Sands.

Port Mulgrave from Lingrow Cliffs.

Our coastal route leaves Whitby by the western pier, dropping down to the beach below the old 12 pounder gun salvaged from the wreck of the steamer *African Transport*. The best way to reach our next destination – Sandsend – is along the beach. It's a wonderful beach and at low tide offers a very attractive alternative to road walking. Technically, The Cleveland Way heads along the top of West Cliff and then along the A174 to Sandsend, but the beach is a much more appealing way to reach the appropriately named Sandsend. It is essential to check the tide times.

At low tide it will be popular with families and walkers with dogs, rock pooling or searching out fossils towards Sandsend Ness. Ichthyosaur bones have been found here and at nearby Kettleness. The route heads across Whitby Sands, Upgang Beach and Sandsend Beach and soon arrives at the small village of Sandsend where a line of Victorian houses sternly face the sea. The wooden skeleton of an old jetty runs across the sand. The view back to Whitby Abbey is grand, as they say around here.

Sandsend is a little gem, particularly the attractive cottages of East Row around Sandsend Beck which trickles into the sea here. Behind is the wooded Mulgrave Estate, open to visitors at weekends and bank holidays.

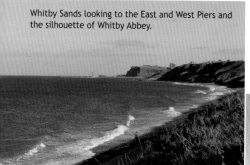

Whitby Sands looking to the East and West Piers and the silhouette of Whitby Abbey.

East Row, Sandsend.

Sandsend from Sandsend Ness.

Whitby from Lythe Bank.

If you're feeling energetic, a climb up the steep Lythe Bank to the churchyard of St Oswald's offers a superb view looking back to Whitby Abbey, but our coastal route continues behind the old railway station, closed in May 1958 and now a residence. The platforms and station building are still in place, but the lattice iron bridge that carried the railway over the road is long dismantled.

The coastal route now joins the cinder trackbed of the old railway line and follows this out to Sandsend Ness where alum was quarried until the 1860s. The exposed workings present a moonlike surface as vegetation has been slow to reclaim this inhospitable terrain. The vegetation is steadily starting to recover in pockets and this is a popular wild spot where roe deer and red fox can be seen. The old railway line twists and turns between boulder clay mounds and in summer heather blazes purple on these hummocks.

Before long the route approaches the sealed tunnel mouth and climbs steeply up through the trees to gain the high ground that climbs out to Keldhowe Steel.

The next part of the route to Kettleness is through typical coastal farmland, a patchwork of fields, a mix of arable crops and dairy and cattle farming.

Sandsend Ness from Sandsend.

The trackbed of the old Staithes to Whitby railway line on Sandsend Ness.

Kettleness from Kettleness Sands.

Kettleness alum workings.

The route winds over Tellgreen Hill, Ovalgate Cliff and on to Seaveybog Hill, a name that crops up in a few places across the moors around here. Passing the old Roman signal station at Goldsborough, it continues into Kettleness. There were five Roman signal stations on the Yorkshire Coast. We passed the first three at Filey Brigg, Scarborough Castle and the Raven Hall Hotel at Ravenscar. The final link in the chain is on Hunt Cliff near Saltburn. Observers would scan the horizon for signs of seaborne raiders and if suspicious craft were spotted, a beacon would be lit and the message could be quickly sent up and down the coastline. Soldiers could then be mobilised quickly to any potential landing sites.

Kettleness is an excellent place for fossil hunting. The Ness is comprised of shale and has been quarried over the years for alum. It's possible to scramble down to the beach on the footpath from Kettleness to Kettleness Sands or to walk in from Runswick Sands, though you must watch the tide times carefully. Ammonites and belemnites are very common here.

Alum was quarried at Kettleness from around 1728 until the late nineteenth century. A huge landslip in December 1829 destroyed many of the houses and part of the alum works. The damage was so extensive that it would be another two years before the alum works reopened.

113

Kettleness from Runswick Sands.

The railway arrived in Kettleness in December 1883 and it would operate through until closure in May 1958. Built by the Whitby, Redcar and Middlesbrough Union Railway, the line connected Whitby to Loftus. It was later absorbed into the North Eastern Railway. The surveyors and navvies had tremendous difficulties engineering a route along this coastline. Work started on a shelf cut into the cliff face, but this collapsed and the engineers had to resort to the more expensive option of two long tunnels. At 308 yards, Kettleness Tunnel was the shorter of the two, with Sandsend Tunnel an impressive 1652 yards long. As well as declining passenger numbers in the 1950s, the challenge and cost of maintaining this heavily engineered route eventually led to the railway's demise.

From Kettleness the coastal path begins the glorious approach to Runswick Bay and drops steadily down to Runswick Sands at Hob Holes where a number of becks drain into the bay.

As with Boggle Hole, Hob Holes is another place where hobgoblins would be found. This particular hobgoblin is reputed to have had the ability to cure whooping cough, a particularly niche talent.

Runswick Bay from High Cliff.

You will need to have arrived at low tide as the path here runs along the beach, which at high tide is likely to be inaccessible. Runswick Bay is another circular bay and the settlement very reminiscent of some of the coastal villages found in Cornwall or North Devon. It's a real hidden gem, rarely busy, with the crowds heading for Whitby, Robin Hood's Bay and Staithes. The village itself nestles into the protective arm of the cliff and is a jumble of cottages and alleyways. The climate must be reasonably mild here because a palm tree grows next to a thatched cottage on the seaward side of the village. This is where Yorkshire vet James Herriot used to holiday.

The village has led a perilous existence. In 1682 a violent storm caused a huge landslip and all houses bar one were lost to the sea. Few lives were lost in the storm and the village was subsequently rebuilt.

There is an old lifeboat station here and a café just above the beach. An old rail-mounted winch recalls the days when fishing cobles were hauled in from the surf onto the sands. It's a steep climb from Runswick Bay to Bank Top and the upper half of the village from where the coastal cliff-top path is regained to head on towards Staithes.

Right: Runswick Bay village.

Below: Runswick Bay lifeboat station.

The lifeboat made national headline news when in 1901 the women of Runswick Bay launched the lifeboat because the men from the village were all out fishing when a storm developed. The women raised the alarm and a small group of farm labourers and older men from the village formed the crew, while the women pushed the lifeboat down the slipway, across the beach and into the sea. The rescue was a success and the men in their fishing boats were assisted back safely home. As a reward for their bravery, the women were invited to a reception and dinner in Manchester and presented with a plaque.

In November 1924 the Runswick lifeboat took part in one of its biggest rescues, helping nineteen crew off the stricken SS *Princess Clementine*.

Runswick Bay village, thatched cottage and palm tree.

Runswick Bay from Kettleness.

Below: Boulby Cliff from Beacon Hill.
Right: Turnstones, Port Mulgrave.

The coastal path continues along the top of Lingrow Cliffs above Wrack Hills and on into Port Mulgrave. On the approach to Port Mulgrave we pass Lingrow Howe, the name suggestive of a burial mound or tumulus, but there is none to be found on the ground. Port Mulgrave itself was a Victorian creation, built to ship iron ore mined locally. The remains of the jetty survive down in the bay.

The port was built by the Grinkle Park Mining Company in 1857 and it operated until 1934. As there was no road access to the quays, a mile long railway tunnel was excavated through the cliff to the port and railway wagons transported the iron ore from the mine at Easington, near to where Boulby's potash mine is today. The iron ore was shipped to Jarrow on Tyneside. The railway was dismantled at the outbreak of the Second World War and the jetty partly demolished to prevent its use by invading German forces.

A few fishing cobles still operate out of the tiny jetty, but it is a steep climb down and back out from the quay.

Beyond Port Mulgrave the path passes below Beacon Hill – another clue as to how vital the high ground was along this coast, yet another link in the chain of signal stations that have been used throughout the ages to communicate messages up and down this dramatic coast. Hinderwell Beacon was an Elizabethan era beacon, rather than the more typical Roman signal stations that line this coast. The principle however is exactly the same. The coastal path now crosses farmland to approach Staithes, dropping down gently to arrive amongst the cottages and onto the quayside.

117

SUGGESTED SHORT WALKS

Staithes and Port Mulgrave   (4 ½ miles / 7.2 km)

This walk visits the charming harbour of Staithes before following the coastal route to the Victorian industrial quay at Port Mulgrave.

From the car park at Staithes head down the steep road down into Staithes and take some time to explore this attractive village with its jumble of cottages.

Head on past the Cod and Lobster public house and then turn right up Church Street and the Mission from which the street takes its name. The cottage claiming to be Captain Cook's cottage is where the famous explorer was apprentice to a draper.

Follow the lane up to its demise and then head uphill with the path on The Cleveland Way that climbs up above the village to a farm.

The Cleveland Way then heads out along the cliff-top path to climb up above Old Nab and then on to arrive into Port Mulgrave. From Port Mulgrave follow the lane into Hinderwell to the junction where you will find St Hilda's church.

A footpath leads from West End Close down across fields to a footbridge in the wooded The Dales. Crossing Dales Beck, turn right to follow a delightful path that climbs high within oak woodland on a ridge. This continues to a footbridge and then joins a track that leads out through Dalehouse to a lane. Turn right to climb steeply up to the main road at Staithes. Cross the main road and follow the lane opposite back to the car park above Staithes village.

Old Nab from Beacon Hill.

Kettleness Chapel and Village.

Runswick Bay and Kettleness (3 ½ miles / 5.5 km)

This is a short walk that offers stunning views to Runswick Bay. You'll need to check tide times for the walk along the beach at Runswick Bay.

Starting from the car park down by the beach in Runswick Bay, the walk climbs steeply up the hill to Runswick Bank top and then turns left at the cross-roads to follow the lane to the point where it crosses the old railway line.

Join the old railway line here to head in a south-easterly direction past Low House Farm and across Coverdale Lane. This railway line ran to Whitby via Staithes, but closed in 1958.

Kettleness from Kettleness Farm.

The railway takes a long loop across Calais Beck before heading back towards the coast near High Cliff. Stay with the old railway line as it runs past the site of the old Kettleness mines. As it approaches the old railway station which is still intact, the route heads right to join a lane where you then turn left.

Join The Cleveland Way here and head east, passing Kettleness Farm to reach the clifftop path. This offers excellent views of Kettle Ness where extensive alum extraction took place and more particularly, stunning views across Runswick Bay to the little fishing village nestling below the headland.

The Cleveland Way drops down from High Cliff to Hob Holes where it follows the beck onto the beach. There then follows a grand stride across the sands, an excellent way to arrive in Runswick Bay. Take some time to explore this charming little village.

Above: Kettleness from Kettleness Sands.
Below: Hob Holes looking out to Runswick Bay.

Sandsend Beach to Whitby.

Looking towards Whitby from the top of Tellgreen Hill.

CHAPTER 11
STAITHES TO SALTBURN

Saltburn Pier.

Staithes from Cowbar Nab.

Traditional Yorkshire cobles, Roxby Beck, Staithes.

High Street, Staithes.

The next leg of the coastal route starts in Staithes, pronounced 'Steers' locally. Staithes is a beautiful little harbour, quaint, characterful and cosy. It's a busy little fishing harbour where traditional Yorkshire cobles still ply their trade, setting crab and lobster pots. Staithes is particularly attractive, whichever way you approach or explore the village. It's a delightful harbour to explore on foot, a real jumble of white-washed cottages, arranged it seems in no particular order, which means there are some fantastic alleyways and stepped ginnels to discover.

There are great views from the top of Cowbar Nab, the huge protective rock and clay outcrop that shelters the harbour and is home to a colony of kittiwakes. Another good vantage point is the footpath that runs at a high level inland from the village, looking down over the red pantile roofs and out to sea. The best view is from the bench once you've climbed steeply up Cowbar Lane to the first row of cottages and it's a great place to rest and absorb the higgledy-piggledy layout of Staithes. There are few house numbers, they all just have names. Staithes also claims one of the narrowest streets in England, a little alley known as Dog Loup.

The attractive old village has attracted artists and painters since the nineteenth century and the village remains popular today with those hoping to capture a sense of its unique atmosphere. As with St Ives on the Cornish coast, the clear sea air helps to create a particularly unique light which these artists seek to capture on canvas.

Roxby Beck, Staithes and the boundary between North Yorkshire and Cleveland, but both sides still firmly in the traditional North Riding!

The Cod and Lobster pub has borne the brunt of many a storm and in 1953 the North Sea breached the windows and swept some of the bottled stock out into the harbour, returning it to the beach days later much to the delight of the beachcombers! On at least one occasion the bow of a boat has come in through the window too!

Cook was actually an apprentice working for a draper when he was based in Staithes in 1744. It is unlikely that the current Captain Cook Cottage had anything to do with James Cook; the place he originally worked in was lost in a violent storm in 1745 when 12 cottages were washed away into the North Sea.

The old railway closed in 1958 and the piers of the viaduct that carried the railway over Roxby Beck can still be seen. What a journey it would be today and how popular as a steam trip.

Roxby Beck which flows into the sea here was the 1974 county boundary between North Yorkshire and Cleveland, but allegiances to the historic North Riding are still strong here and as far as most folk are concerned, this is all Yorkshire.

Traditional Yorkshire cobles, Roxby Beck, Staithes.

North of Staithes The Cleveland Way takes the old Cowbar Lane, sections of which have now been lost to coastal erosion and a new lane for road traffic has been built further inland. How long before this too succumbs to the advancing attentions of the North Sea?

The surface buildings of Boulby Potash Mine soon come into view. Boulby Mine was opened in 1974 to exploit potash both from below ground and under the sea. Boulby Mine has been used by scientists for the study of Dark Matter. This is because it is the deepest mine in Europe, extending 1 mile below sea level with mine levels that radiate 5 miles out to sea. That means it is as dark as it's possible to get underground! Potash is used as a fertiliser and in the steel and chemical industry. Salt is also extracted as a by-product and is used for road gritting.

Beyond the mine are Boulby Cliffs, the highest sea cliffs on the East coast of England. Rising 666 feet above sea level they offer a superb vantage point to look back towards Staithes. The Vikings named this part of the coastline Cleveland – "land of the cliffs". It's a good pull to the trig point at 213 metres above sea level above Rock Cliff. The buttery smell of flowering gorse is a heady aroma through much of spring and summer. The cliff section between here and Gallihowe was originally used to quarry alum, along with similar quarries at Kettleness, Ravenscar and Sandsend Ness.

Right: Boulby Cliff from Cowbar Nab.

Below: Looking down on Staithes from Boulby Cliff.

From here The Cleveland Way continues across the tops of Hummersea Bank with Hummersea Scar exposed at low tide below. The high ground affords great views across the valley where tiny Skinningrove village nestles and Kilton Beck joins the North Sea.

Skinningrove is a former mining and steel village and the steelworks on Carlin How is still there today up above the village. The beck that runs in to the sea here betrays the ironstone seams below ground, the water a distinct orange colour as a result of the iron content. Ironstone was discovered here in 1847 and the tiny village quickly developed to support the burgeoning iron industry. Skinningrove is also home to the Cleveland Mining Museum. A few fishing cobles can be found dragged up on the beach.

A redundant concrete jetty gives an indication as to the former importance of this natural harbour.

Beyond the jetty is the delightful Cattersty Sands, a lovely section of golden beach below the towering Cattersty Cliffs. A brief climb brings you to the top of the cliffs and ahead is Warsett Hill. There are two Warsett Hills acting as guardians either side of the deep gorge that holds Kilton Beck.

Right: Cattersty Sands and Hummersea Cliff from Cattersty Cliff.

Below: Cattersty Sands and Skinningrove harbour from Hummersea Cliff.

Saltburn from Hunt Cliff.

Here the coastal path runs tightly between the railway and the cliff top. The railway itself runs perilously close to the cliff top and was built in 1867 to serve the ironstone mines that were being developed just inland around Boulby. The line closed to passengers in May 1960 and is now used by freight trains serving the steelworks at Skinningrove and potash mine at Boulby. There are very occasional steam-hauled excursions to Boulby.

Steam locomotive No.61994 *The Great Marquess* works a special train across Hunt Cliff en-route from Middlesbrough to Boulby.

The cliffs here were used by the Romans as a signal station, one of a series of signal stations or beacons to allow rapid transmittal of messages up and down Britain's Roman occupied East Coast. The Roman signal station on Hunt Cliff is thought to date back to around AD350 and research suggests it operated for about fifty years before being destroyed. Excavations on site revealed 14 mutilated bodies dumped in an old well and this has led archaeologists to conclude that a raid took place here, possibly by Angles from Northern Europe.

Kittiwakes can again be found nesting here on Hunt Cliff and by now the grand view has opened out to Saltburn down below, with wide sandy beaches and the first pier since Whitby.

Saltburn is a classic Victorian coastal resort and it nestles down in the valley against a backdrop of towering blast furnaces and the coking plants of industrial Redcar and South Bank on Teesside.

Before it was developed as a Victorian seaside town, Saltburn was a small village surviving on fishing and salt panning. This gave Saltburn its name, the village was located where Skelton Beck – the 'burn' - runs into the sea.

Saltburn was created in the 1860s when the railway arrived from nearby Redcar. It was the work of Henry Pease, a devout Quaker who had acquired his wealth in the iron industry and as a director of the Stockton and Darlington Railway Company. Pease saw the potential of Saltburn as a seaside resort to attract the ironworkers from his Teesside ironworks.

It was Pease that brought the railway to Saltburn, originally terminating next to the Zetland Hotel. A company was formed to develop the resort – the Saltburn Improvement Company – and they were responsible for the grand houses on Marine Drive. The railway still serves Saltburn today bringing daytrippers from Middlesbrough and Darlington. Saltburn is useful for bus links too.

Saltburn Pier is the last surviving pleasure pier on the Yorkshire coast. It was built in 1869 and when first opened it was nearly 500 yards long. As with the other piers on the East Coast, it has since been much curtailed, largely due to collisions with shipping traffic, the first being the *Ovenbeg* which struck the pier in 1924. Further damage was caused during the Second World War and soon after heavy storm damage in 1952 reduced the length of the pier further still. After further storm damage in 1974, its fate hung in the balance, but a concerted local campaign led to its restoration and today it remains a splendid addition to Saltburn's attractions.

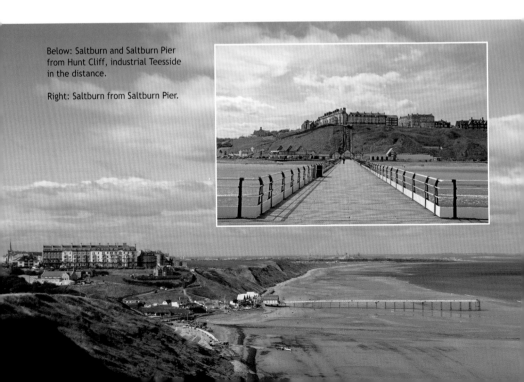

Below: Saltburn and Saltburn Pier from Hunt Cliff, industrial Teesside in the distance.

Right: Saltburn from Saltburn Pier.

The Cliff Lift is water powered and was opened in 1884. It replaced a vertical hoist and employs an ingenious method to power the cars. A water tank on top of each car is filled until the weight of the upper car reaches the tipping point at which point it starts to descend the cliff. The brake is operated from the upper cabin. Both cars are connected by a steel cable and the weight of the descending car hauls the lower car to the top. The water tank at the bottom is emptied while that of the car at the top is filled and the process repeats itself. An excellent early example of environmentally friendly transport!

Saltburn Cliff Lift, upper station.

Saltburn Cliff Lift and Saltburn Pier.

It's also worth seeking out the Saltburn Miniature Railway just in the park. This 15 inch gauge railway opened in 1947 and was further extended in 1953. It is now run by volunteers and offers a hark back to a simpler age when a holiday on the coast was the main family holiday of the year.

Saltburn Sands offer a wonderful place to stride out – 'bracing' – to borrow a phrase from the old Skegness railway poster. A popular place to exercise dogs and for families in summer, old tractors can be found up and down the beach which are used to haul the small fleet of crabbing boats in and out of the surf. Between 1908 and the 1930s, Saltburn Sands was used for motor racing and some of the top racing drivers of the day came here to race their cars. Malcolm Campbell drove his famous *Bluebird* on the sands here.

The Ship Inn nestles below Hunt Cliff and is thought to date back to 1550. A character called John Andrew was landlord of the Ship Inn in the 1780s. He earned the title 'The King of the Smugglers'. Smuggling was rife all along the Yorkshire Coast, particularly during the eighteenth and nineteenth centuries. It seems that almost everyone was involved. Wealthy landowners would finance some of the purchases and the local fishermen were involved in landing contraband goods. The local villagers would help to unload the goods from the boats and squirrel it away in hideaways, caves, coves, cellars and pits. The local pannier men would have helped to transport the goods into villages and towns to be sold and of course shopkeepers would almost certainly and knowingly have sold the contraband on. It's a wonder that they all managed to keep it a secret. Smuggling wasn't limited to alcohol, smuggling was all about avoiding paying a higher price for highly taxed goods and so it could be anything from silk, to chocolate, to tea and snuff.

Below: The Ship Inn, Old Saltburn.

Right: Vintage tractor in use to launch crabbing boat, Saltburn Sands.

Cliff House, built by Henry Pease and Hunt Cliff from Marske-by-the-Sea.

It is an irony that the coastguard cottages built here to try and stop the smuggling trade were built directly above the Ship Inn, probably to send a clear message that the activity there was being constantly watched from above!

As with Cayton Bay further south, Saltburn has a burgeoning surfing culture with high rollers coming in direct from the North Sea.

This is where The Cleveland Way turns inland to follow the North York Moors northern escarpment on its journey to Helmsley and this is where we'll take our leave of the Yorkshire Coast. The sections beyond to Redcar and Gare Point merge with the Tees Estuary and this seems like a fitting point at which to turn around and do it all again heading south, or catch a bus or train with tired legs and head for home, ready to tackle another section another day.

Marske Sands and industrial Teesside from Saltburn-by-the-Sea.

SUGGESTED SHORT WALKS

Saltburn and Hunt Cliff   (3 ½ miles / 5.5km)

This short walk climbs high above Saltburn to Hunt Cliff where kittiwakes nest. It offers a good opportunity to appraise Saltburn from on high against a backdrop of industrial Teesside.

From the top of Saltburn's Cliff Lift take the steps down to the promenade and head right along the road, crossing Skelton Beck to arrive in Old Saltburn. The Ship Inn and Saltburn Smugglers Experience can be found nestling below the cliffs.

Take the bridleway that climbs up past the former coastguard cottages to Ladgates Farm. Ahead is the shapely outline of Warsett Hill. At a crossroads of paths, turn left to head straight for the coast. On arrival at the cliff top turn right along The Cleveland Way on the clifftop path to Hunt Cliff. There is a plaque indicating

the site of the former Roman Signal Station, one of a chain on the Yorkshire Coast.

We turn around here and follow The Cleveland Way back along the cliff top path downhill back to the Ship Inn and Old Saltburn.

Left: Saltburn Cliff Lift, bottom station.

Below: The old Zetland Hotel, Saltburn-by-the-Sea.

Sea fret, Gallihowe.

Hummersea Cliff and Scar from Gallihowe, with Cattersty Sands beyond.

Hummersea   (4 miles / 6.17 km)

This walk embraces the industrial heritage of the Yorkshire Coast. We start in Skinningrove which still retains a working steel mill.

From the bridge which crosses Kilton Beck close to where it discharges into the sea, take The Cleveland Way steeply uphill on the coastal path above Hummersea Cliff. This climbs energetically up to Hummersea Point, a grand place to pause and look back to enjoy the view down to Skinningrove and across to Cattersty.

The route continues on The Cleveland Way as it climbs ever higher above Hummersea Bank to pass through a farm and then above The Warren. As we reach the top we have a clear view below of the disturbance caused by alum quarrying on the cliff slopes.

From here we double back right on a footpath that heads across fields to join the lane that climbs from Micklow Hill to Upton Hill.

We turn right along this lane and keep right where it forks. As the road bends right, our footpath continues on downhill to Deepdale Farm and Hummersea Lane. We cross straight over to join Cleveland Street – a long distance route that crosses the undulating countryside that nestles behind the coastline. Our way now keeps with Cleveland Street and follows it down into Skinningrove arriving at the Cleveland Ironstone Mining Museum. The museum offers a fascinating insight into the history of ironstone mining in the area. Ironstone mining ceased in 1958, but the production of iron and steel continued into the 1970s. Although parts of the steelworks remain in use, the mill is now used for rolling steel.

From here we turn right on the lane to head back to the start.

Hummersea Cliff and Scar from Gallihowe.

Cattersty Sands from the old jetty at Skinningrove.

CHAPTER 12
BEST OF THE REST: SPURN POINT TO BARMSTON

Coastal erosion on the boulder clay cliffs, Hornsea.

Coastal erosion on the cliffs between Hornsea and Mappleton.

Spurn Point's 1895-built lighthouse.

Spurn Point is where the Yorkshire Coast begins or ends, depending on your point of view. Today Spurn is a National Nature Reserve managed by the Yorkshire Wildlife Trust, an important wintering ground for migrating birds and a fascinating geological feature. Created and extended as a result of longshore drift from coastal erosion further north on Holderness , Spurn Point is ever changing.

During the medieval period, Spurn Point was a pivotal point for two insurrections against the ruling monarchy, first in 1399 when Henry of Bolingbroke landed as part of his campaign to usurp Richard II. Later in 1471, Martin de la See organised local resistance against the landing of Edward IV on his return to England from exile in Holland.

The villages on Spurn that were at the heart of these dramatic events no longer exist; coastal erosion has seen Spurn migrate steadily westwards over time.

The most recent change came in December 2013 when a huge tidal surge, the result of strong north-easterly winds and exceptionally high tides, overwhelmed large sections of the Yorkshire and Lincolnshire coast. The tide breached the old access road and today there is no vehicular access to the Point. At high tide Spurn becomes Yorkshire's only island.

Access on foot is still possible, but it is vital to plan any visit on foot around the tide times. The Yorkshire Wildlife Trust operates regular Spurn Safaris in their four-wheel-drive Unimog. This offers an excellent opportunity to visit the birdlife from a mobile hide and to take a trip to the newly refurbished lighthouse.

There have been lighthouses on Spurn since the seventeenth century and the principle of maintaining a high light and a low light was established then. Two new lighthouses were built in 1767, but coastal erosion continued to undermine the low light. A replacement was built in 1852 and this is the low light that still stands on the beach today. In 1895 the modern lighthouse we see today was built and this replaced the need for both a low and high light. This lighthouse was designed by Thomas Matthews with a range of 17 nautical miles. It was made redundant in 1985 and remained empty until fully refurbished in 2015.

There was once a lightship stationed 4 miles off Spurn Point. These are vessels without engines and a small light tower installed. They were towed into position and then anchored in vulnerable locations to provide additional warning for shipping traffic. Today the Spurn lightship is preserved at Hull. It was built in 1927 and withdrawn from service in 1975.

Spurn protects the mouth of the River Humber, an important shipping lane and still particularly busy today with ships serving the large ports at Immingham and Hull. A lifeboat station was built at Spurn in 1810 and still operates today. Due to its remote location, houses for the lifeboat crew were built next to the lifeboat station and it remains the only lifeboat station with full time paid staff.

Left: The Spurn lightship now preserved at Hull Humber Dock.

Below: Spurn Point's 1852-built low light with the 1895 built replacement on the right.

Withernsea's redundant pier entrance towers.

Withernsea lighthouse.

Spurn Point has long been recognised as of strategic importance throughout history. During the First World War a number of defensive structures were built to protect the mouth of the River Humber and the remains of gun emplacements can still be found today. A railway was built in 1915 to service the wartime defences and the tracks remain visible in places, particularly around the lighthouse. Sail-driven railway trucks were used, given the exposed location, a novel means of motive power. Traditional steam locomotives were also stationed on the point.

Withernsea's short lived pier was built in 1877 and stretched nearly 400 yards out into the sea, but it was regularly struck by ships. The first collision came in 1880, followed quickly in 1888 and 1893 by which time the truncated remains were an embarrassing 50 feet of pier! The pier was therefore dismantled and today the sandstone towers that marked the entrance are preserved as part of Withernsea's promenade.

Withernsea lighthouse was built inland in the centre of the town in 1894. Like most of our coastal lighthouses, it was owned and operated by Trinity House until closure came in 1976. Today the lighthouse is home to a museum and still presents an incongruous sight amongst the streets and terraces of Withernsea.

Hornsea developed as a Victorian seaside resort when the Hull and Hornsea Railway arrived in 1864. The town has a strong Georgian atmosphere in the buildings around the cobbled church of St Nicholas. The railway lasted for 100 years and like its near neighbour Withernsea, Hornsea has declined in the last fifty years as a seaside resort. Nearby Hornsea Mere is the largest natural lake in Yorkshire. Today Hornsea is the beginning or end of The Transpennine Trail which heads across country to the Lancashire coast at Southport.

SUGGESTED SHORT WALKS

Skipsea and Withow Gap   (1 ¼ miles / 2.1 km)

This is a very short walk on a permissive path that explores the wartime defences installed during the Second World War to protect this vulnerable stretch of coastline. It's also an opportunity to appreciate the coastal erosion that takes place on the Holderness coast.

The walk starts from the car park of Mr Moo's ice cream parlour. Famous around the East Riding, if you leave your car here, please make sure you sample the local ice cream at the beginning or end of your walk.

A permissive path leaves the car park to strike north through an orchard of trees and then turns right to follow a grassy path beside a small drainage channel through rolling fields to Withow Gap.

Fossilised beaver dam, Skipsea.

On the way two wartime pillboxes are passed, a large typical 'lozenge' shaped pillbox and a smaller square concrete construction. The larger pillbox located on higher ground known as The Hold clearly had a sweeping field of fire. A cold war-era Royal Observer Corps bunker is also located adjacent to the permissive path, along with a First World War bunker.

Boulder clay cliffs, Skipsea.

The path terminates at Withow Gap where it is easy to access the beach and take some time to appraise the boulder clay cliffs. These are constantly changing and eroding as the North Sea bites chunks out of the Yorkshire coastline during winter storms. The boulder clays readily give up fossils and in recent years an old beaver dam has been revealed at Withow Gap. This beaver dam dates back about 10,000 years to the end of the Ice Age and has been preserved under layers of silt. This area used to be a freshwater mere, similar to nearby Hornsea mere, but over time became covered in deposits which preserved the timbers of the ancient trees used by the beavers to build the dam.

The route retraces the outward journey to the car park and ice cream parlour. An interesting diversion is the motte and bailey castle in Skipsea, currently in the care of English Heritage.

Left: Second World War pillbox, Skipsea.

Below: Coastal erosion of boulder clay cliffs, Skipsea.

Hornsea sunrise.

BIBLIOGRAPHY

East Yorkshire Curiosities Robert Woodhouse History Press (2010)
The Buildings of England: North Riding Nikolaus Pevsner Yale (2002)
The Buildings of England: East Riding Nikolaus Pevsner Yale (2005)
Prehistoric Rock Art in the North York Moors Paul Brown and Graeme Chappell
                                                    History Press (2012)
Railways Around Whitby Vol.1 Martin Bairstow Bairstow (1998)
Railways Around Whitby Vol.2 Martin Bairstow Bairstow (1996)
Fossils of the Whitby Coast Dean Lomax Siri (2011)
Yorkshire Coast and North York Moors Lisa Pritchard Myriad (2009)
Lost Railways of North & East Yorkshire Gordon Suggitt Countryside Books (2005)
Cleveland Way Ian Sampson Aurum (2012)
Yorkshire Coastline Ian Smith Sandhill Press (1990)
North York Moors and Yorkshire Wolds Mike Bradshaw Bradt (2014)
North York Moors Brian Conduit Jarrold (1998)
Vale of York and Yorkshire Wolds Brian Conduit Jarrold (2002)
East Yorkshire Pocket Pub Walks Sally Burnard Countryside Books (2012)
Short Walks in the North York Moors Brian Spencer Collins (2013)
North York Moors Dan Kelsall Crimson (2009)
Walks Around the Yorkshire Coast Malcolm Boyes Dalesman (2008)

INDEX